FOREWORD TO THE THIRD EDITION

The Mountains to Sound Greenway Trust is proud to join the Mountaineers in a third printing of Yvonne Prater's wonderful history of Snoqualmie Pass.

The story of the pass is as fascinating as the scenic treasure itself. First Nation Americans, immigrant settlers, miners, cattlemen, and railroad builders created this route across the Cascade Mountains. Ms. Prater has mined rich veins of early events and pioneer people. Writing in the 1970s, she was able to record first hand accounts from men and women who watched each stage of development at the pass in the last century.

In 1909, 105 cars crossed the pass on the one-lane dirt and gravel "sunset highway." They hardly gave a hint of the more than 20 million people who now cross the pass in motor vehicles each year. The one-lane road has become a major interstate freeway and the Greenway segment has been designated a National Scenic Byway.

The Greenway Trust is working to preserve and mark many of the historic places described in this book. In cooperation with other civic groups, landowners, cities, counties, the State of Washington, and the U.S. Forest Service, the Trust is also stimulating the public purchase of key resource lands, the reopening of historic paths, and the development of new trails and scenic view sites. We also encourage cities and towns along the Greenway to maintain their historic identities and to strengthen their economies in ways which respect their natural settings.

A wise historian has said that each of us is partnered with the past and the future in a process that makes us who we are. The Greenway Trust hopes these stories of historic Snoqualmie Pass inspire readers to help protect this special place for future generations.

After reading Ms. Prater's book, you are likely to discover that your next trip across the pass will have mysteriously become more exciting.

Enjoy!

Jim Ellis
President Emeritus, Mountains to Sound Greenway Trust
June 2008

For other information about the Greenway's gradual realization, refer to Daniel Chasan's book, *Mountains to Sound, the Creation of a Greenway across the Cascades*, and visit the Greenway website at *www.mtsgreenway.org* to access Jim Ellis' speeches *Take the Greenway* (1991), and *The Road Still Beckons* (2006).

Peaks around Snoqualmie Pass rise above Lake Keechelus in this early-1930s view.

SNOQUALMIE PASS

From Indian Trail to Interstate

Yvonne Prater

THE MOUNTAINEERS BOOKS
*is the nonprofit publishing arm of The Mountaineers Club, an organization
founded in 1906 and dedicated to the exploration, preservation, and enjoyment
of outdoor and wilderness areas.*
www.mountaineers.org

THE MOUNTAINS TO SOUND GREENWAY TRUST
*Organized in 1991 to protect forests, farms, parks, trails, wildlife habitat,
outdoor recreation, environmental education opportunities and history in a
100-mile corridor along Interstate 90 from Seattle to Central Washington.*
www.mtsgreenway.org

Published by
The Mountaineers
1001 SW Klickitat Way, Suite 201
Seattle, WA 98134

Reprintings by
The Mountains to Sound Greenway Trust
911 Western Avenue, Suite 523
Seattle, WA 98104

First printing 1981, second printing 1995, third printing 2008

Manufactured in the United States of America

Cover design by The Mountaineers Books
Book design by Barbara Haner
Maps by Gray Mouse Graphics

Front cover photograph: *Snoqualmie Pass, 1920s* Photo courtesy of Special Collections, Suzzallo
   Library, University of Washington
Back cover photograph: *The Milwaukee Road railway brought electric trains across Snoqualmie
   Pass on several trestles in the Cascades, including this one above Hall Creek that was rebuilt in
   1999 by Washington State Parks as part of the John Wayne Pioneer Trail. Mountains to Sound
   Greenway volunteers regularly maintain and improve this trail, the backbone of the Greenway
   regional trail system.* Photo by Milwaukee Road

Library of Congress Cataloging-in-Publication Data

Prater, Yvonne, 1932–
   Snoqualmie Pass.
   Bibliography; p.
   Includes index.
   1. Snoqualmie Pass (Wash.) —History. I. title.
HE356.W3P7   1981   979.7'57   81-16911
ISBN 978-0-89886-015-3   AACR2

To Mark

ACKNOWLEDGMENTS

I wish to extend a special "thank you" to the following individuals and organizations who contributed valuable help in the form of research, comments, inspiration, and original history through interviews and old photographs. I especially appreciate the encouragement and support of my husband, Gene, and our children through years of data gathering.

My thanks go to Jeanne Engerman, Frank Green, and Pat Brahmen, Washington State Historical Society Library, Tacoma; Susan Carter, Wenatchee National Forest research archaeologist; Glenda Madole, Automobile Club of Washington; Mary Thadia d'Hondt, Museum of History and Industry, Seattle; Jill Rockwell, Yakima Regional Library; Morris Jenkins, Jessica (Bull) Short, Bob Monahan, Jim Heckman, Mary Farrell, Snoqualmie Valley Historical Society and Museum, North Bend; Andrew Johnson, Pacific Northwest Collection, Suzzallo Library, University of Washington, Seattle; Tom Lyon, Ron Selstead, Steve Morse, Sam Talerico, Charles Fowler, Jake Krahenbuhl, Ted Clerf, Robert Lanphere, Daws Roberts, Joe Graham, Ray Neuman, and Harold Garrett, Washington State Department of Transportation; Joan Peter, Tobias Notenboom, Dallas Van Horn, Susan Stump, Paul Frankenstein, Ken White, and Paul Hart, United States Forest Service.

I owe a great deal also to Wilbur Helm, Yakima Genealogical Society; Jeanne Nashem and Bill Pugh, Yakima Valley Museum; Onni Perala, United States Bureau of Reclamation, Yakima; Jim Scribbens, Milwaukee Railroad; Kathryn Hamilton and Nancy Pryor, Washington State Library, Olympia; Lieutenant Les Dewey, Glen Cramer, Bill Ford, and Sergeant Bob McBride, Washington State Patrol; Webb Moffatt; Ray Tanner; Jack and Wilma Preston; John and Tillie Bresko; Al and Dorothy Scott; Frank Musso, Roslyn Museum; Al Schober, Cle Elum Museum; Edna Fleming; Elna Mason; Harry Weaver; Maxine Kristensen; Fred Krueger; Bea Buzzetti; Bob Ballard; Joe Schnebly; Phillip Paul; Ray Lilleby; John Horan; Ruby Grandstaff; Clara and Jo Wasson; Clovis and Ruth Chartrand; Bob

Say, Kittitas County Road Department; Larry Nickel, Kittitas County Historical Museum; David Wheeler; Bill Speidel; Verna Ness, librarian and publications assistant, The Mountaineers, Seattle; and Mae Anderson, College Club, Seattle.

More thanks go to Andrew Mitchell Library, Aberdeen, South Dakota; Bob Pace, Media Service Center, Yakima Tribal Nation, Toppenish; Snoqualmie Tribal Organization, Issaquah; Kim Holien, Department of Army, Center of Military History, Washington, D.C.; Jim Flatness, Geography and Map Division, Library of Congress, Washington, D.C.; Bob Johnson and Robert Brittain, King County Road Department, Seattle; Gene Halvorsen; Carol Schroeder; Cathy Heaverlo; Jack Bull; George Fadenrecht, Ruth Hartman and Roger Stark, Central Washington University librarians, Ellensburg; Kittitas County Commissioner Roy Lumaco and former Commissioners Carl Ooka and Joe McManamy; Bob Lince and George Martin, Yakima Historical Society; Carolyn Willberg, Glenna Beardsley, Mary James, Ellensburg Library; and Glen Lindemann, History Department, Washington State University.

Others who were helpful were Vance Orchard, Walla Walla *Union Bulletin*; Randy Gregory, Ford Smith, Kent Richards, Central Washington University History Department, Ellensburg; Mike Music, Navy and Old Army Archives, Washington, D.C.; Jim Leyersapf, Eisenhower Library, Abilene, Kansas; Mac Dunbar; North Central Regional Library and Wenatchee Junior College Library, Wenatchee; *Seattle Times* photo morgue; Rod Slemmons, Curator, Whatcom County Museum of History and Art, Bellingham; Hubert Howe Bancroft Library, University of California, Berkeley; Don Colwell; Harry Masterson; Dominic Contratto; Clareta Smith; Cliff Kaynor; Leslie Dameron; Oregon Historical Society, Portland, Oregon; Seattle, Redmond, and Auburn public libraries.

Contents

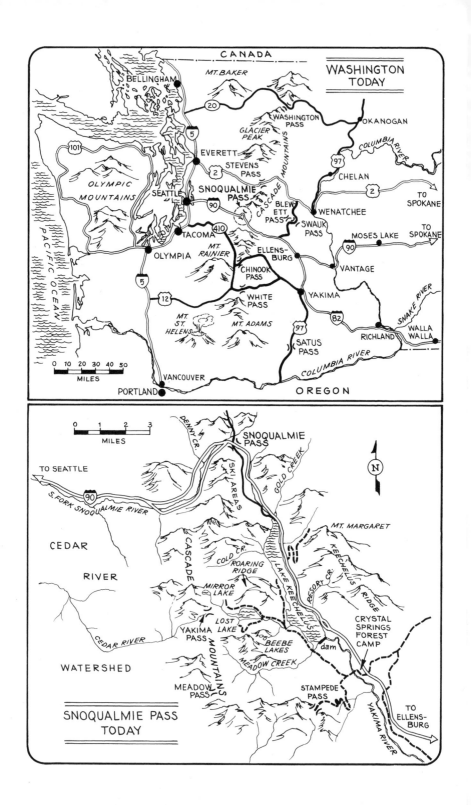

Preface

The paved highway that now crosses Snoqualmie Pass once provided passage through the Cascade Mountains of Washington as an Indian trail, a military and cattle-drive trail, and finally as a wagon road. Where once perhaps a few dozen people traveled in a year's time, now hundreds pass by in an hour. Snoqualmie Pass is one of the most heavily used mountain transportation routes in the United States, and the growth of this road parallels the growth of the region, making the present-day highway an intimate part of Northwest history. After all the changes that have occurred, it is a wonder there are any traces left of the old routes. The region has seen floods and fires; railroad, dam, road, and powerline construction; and the drastic changes brought about by logging.

On the west side of Snoqualmie Pass, the Forest Service, with the help of the Boy Scouts and others, has preserved a one-mile section of the original wagon road, which was laboriously hacked out about 1868 along the route of an Indian trail. Until recently, I thought nothing else remained of the early pioneer routes. Then I discovered Morris Jenkins, a long-time resident of the area who worked as a forester and trapper in the Snoqualmie Pass area, along with working on the highway itself. He remembered running across remnants of the trail thirty or forty years ago and thought we might be able to find them again.

On a beautiful October day, he took me up above Lake Keechelus, east of the pass, his pickup climbing the switchbacks through logging areas on the shoulders of Mount Margaret. When we reached a saddle near an unnamed pond, he parked, pointed up a steep, logged-off ridge, and said, "If there's anything left, we might find a segment of the trail up on top some-where."

At the top of the ridge, we separated in hopes of finding the trail faster. I headed diagonally along the hill and sensed, rather than saw, that I was cutting across an old, old, tread. I stood on it and looked to one side and then the other, then called out, "Come over here. I think I found it."

We walked east, following the tread toward Resort Creek until

it disappeared in a selectively logged area. Jenkins discovered ancient tree blazes that I would never have noticed. Around on the southeast side of Keechelus Ridge, near where the trail disappeared under a logging road, we found huge old trees, never logged, whose trunks had grown sixty to eighty feet since the blazes had been made. The section was probably one-half to three-quarters of a mile in length.

We actually found and walked on the trail, touched the trees

Left, *the road along Lake Keechelus in the 1920s.*
Below, *almost the same stretch in 1981.*

Washington State Historical Society

Yvonne Prater photo

where the blazes were marked; we were careful to photograph it all in case the trail was not there the following year. In the background I could hear a chain saw growling and whining on the edge of a big clearcut, and I wondered how long the route of the ancient trail could last against the speed of modern logging methods.

Two weeks later Jenkins and I again drove west from Cle Elum toward Snoqualmie Pass on the freeway, then turned south at the Stampede Pass interchange and west around the foot of Lake Keechelus and the dam. This time we would be driving as close as we could to the ancient Indian trail that might be still visible in the vicinity of Yakima Pass. We had to leave the vehicle at the road junction at Lost Lake because of a logging gate. We hiked up a hill and around a bend and were in the stream drainage that serves as the outlet to the Beebe Lakes.

Pointing to a big clearcut in the canyon below us, Jenkins explained, "This is the canyon the Indians used to travel from Lake Keechelus, past Beebe Lakes and on to Yakima Pass." He pointed out a place that used to be an Indian campsite deep in the canyon, in the middle of the clearcut, and said, "They've done a lot of logging in here since I first came. I used to use the old Indian trail on my trapline up Roaring Ridge. All the old-time trappers used it and they were the ones who showed it to me. On the edge of where the Indians camped were three 'squaw trees.'"

We dropped down into the canyon to take a look at them but they were now just stumps, having been logged. I asked him what he knew about squaw trees, and he said, "Not much, except that where I came from in Idaho, there were girdled ponderosa pines scattered all through the forest. The Indians would never completely girdle a tree as that would kill it, but they peeled off the bark and chewed it. Apparently, what they liked chewing was the cambium layer underneath the bark. It's turpentine. I've chewed the bark myself. It's chewy, pleasant to the taste, but kind of rubbery." These stripped trees were probably called "squaw trees" because it was primarily the women who did the peeling.

We climbed the forested hillside above the logging road and soon were on the Indian trail — the authentic, ancient route of generations of Indians who migrated back and forth through the Cascade Mountains. How exciting to follow it up a small cliff and visualize a large group of Indians coming straight down that very steep path — single file, on horseback and afoot. It was still a

one-foot-deep trough, in places half-hidden by clumps of pine
grass, turning brown. To be able to set foot on that pathway was
a real treat. If it can ever be preserved, rules will be needed so
that people can walk only ten feet on either side of it, but not on
it. With today's hoards of sightseeing hikers, it would wear out in
a week or get so deep that it would become impassable.

Once again, I went home wondering how much longer these
remnants of Northwest history could survive without protection.
I wanted to know more about the people who struggled through
these dense forests and left us these traces of their passage. I
stayed home from the trail and went instead to the library, where
I found such quantities of information that the complete story
would be a massive volume. I have chosen here to give glimpses
of our past to intrigue the reader.

Something that intrigued me — I never saw it in print — was
the idea that the Snoqualmie Pass route through the Washington
Cascades may be said to be a portion of the "northern branch" of
the Oregon Trail. In reading Northwest history, it becomes obvi-
ous that lack of a wagon road through the Cascades was one of
the reasons Oregon Territory residents living north of the Columbia River petitioned Congress for separate status as Washington Territory, thus concentrating power for promoting their
own, more local interests.

This thought, as well as a growing admiration for the determi-
nation and vision of the several generations who finally achieved
the long-sought transportation route, was with me as I re-
searched through community histories, diaries, newspaper files,
maps, photo collections, and family albums, and conducted personal interviews with the old-timers who made the history. This
book is not a scholarly rendition of past history; rather it's intended as "recreational reading" for those who know, or would
know, Snoqualmie Pass. If the reader enjoys these stories,
perhaps next year I'll not be alone in exploring Snoqualmie's
historic paths.

Yvonne Prater

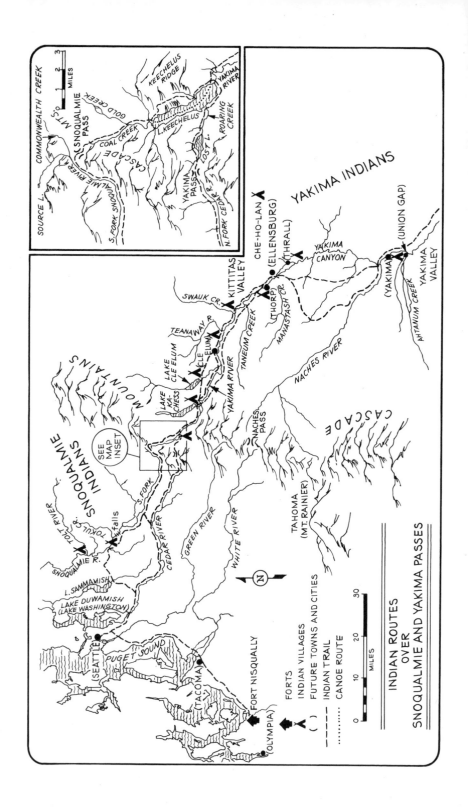

INDIAN ROUTES
OVER
SNOQUALMIE AND YAKIMA PASSES

FORTS
INDIAN VILLAGES
( ) FUTURE TOWNS AND CITIES
— — — INDIAN TRAIL
·········· CANOE ROUTE

MILES
0   10   20   30

YAKIMA INDIANS

SNOQUALMIE INDIANS

CASCADE MOUNTAINS

(SEATTLE)
(TACOMA)
(OLYMPIA)
FORT NISQUALLY
PUGET SOUND

TAHOMA
(MT. RAINIER)

WHITE RIVER
GREEN RIVER
CEDAR RIVER
S. FORK
TOKUL CR.
falls
SNOQUALMIE R.
TOLT RIVER
L. SAMMAMISH
LAKE DUWAMISH
(LAKE WASHINGTON)

SEE MAP INSET

LAKE KA-CHESS
LAKE CLE-ELUM
CLE ELUM
TEANAWAY R.
SWAUK CR.
YAKIMA RIVER
TANEUM CREEK
NACHES PASS
NACHES RIVER
MANASTASH CR.

KITTITAS VALLEY
CHE-HO-LAN
(ELLENSBURG)
(THRALL)
YAKIMA CANYON
(THORP)
(YAKIMA)
(UNION GAP)
AHTANUM CREEK
YAKIMA VALLEY

N

— Inset map —

SOURCE L.
COMMONWEALTH CREEK
ALME RIVER
S. FORK SNOQUALMIE R.
CASCADE MTS.
SNOQUALMIE PASS
COAL CREEK
GOLD CREEK
KEECHELUS RIDGE
L. KEECHELUS
YAKIMA RIVER
ROARING CREEK
LOST L.
YAKIMA PASS
CEDAR R.
N. FORK CEDAR R.

MILES
0   1   2   3

1

Indian Trail

At approximately the same time that the Puget Sound lobe of the Cordilleran ice sheet was digging out Puget Sound and Lakes Washington, Union, and Sammamish, and diverting the Cedar River from its old course of joining the Snoqualmie River, deep alpine glaciers were scouring out mountain valleys. Glaciers formed in the basins of what is now Source Lake and Commonwealth Creek, merged at the base of Guye Peak, flowed down to Snoqualmie Pass, and split, one tongue moving west and the other east. The eastern tongue flowed farthest, almost to the present-day town of Thorp. It gouged out Lake Keechelus and deepened the canyon of the Yakima River. Other tongues flowed from the crest of the Cascades and gouged out Lakes Kachess and Cle Elum, feeding into the glacier in the Yakima River canyon. Ages later, Indian campsites — and later, white development — sprang up along these water routes through the mountains.

It is not known how long ago the Indians discovered this gap in the mountains. Nearby archaeological excavations of ancient living sites on the Enumclaw Plateau to the south show human activity there 6,000 years ago. The Marmes Man site along the Snake River reveals human habitation stretching back at least 10,000 years in eastern Washington. And the Manis mastodon site near Sequim on the Olympic Peninsula suggests that humans were in that area of Washington as much as 12,000 years ago.

Indians on both sides of the Cascades had to be mobile to gather the foods that nature provided with each season. Coastal Indians could rely mainly on fishing in salt water and gathering seafood from the shore, but they also dug roots and hunted. In addition to their base villages with houses made of cedar planks, they had temporary camps of mat-covered shelters in the summer, which were moved from place to place as they headed to the mountains to pick huckleberries and hunt mountain goat. They used the trail across the mountains mainly for trade, but they also used portions of it in these annual trips to the mountains to hunt, gather roots, pick berries, and gather for basket weaving, items that grew only at higher elevations. During the period for which we have any records, the main users of the trail were the Snoqualmies and the Yakimas.

The Snoqualmie Indians lived immediately to the west of the pass. They had an interior coastal culture and spoke the Salish

Yakima Indian braves in ceremonial dress typical of the 1910s. Man at right is identified as Willie John.

McWharter collection

lingual type. One source says the Snoqualmie name means "plenty of waters."

The Snoqualmies traded frequently with Indians of the interior plateau country, using the trail to move back and forth through the Cascades. They had villages along the Snoqualmie River just below the falls of the same name, at Fall City, and at the confluence of the Tolt and Snoqualmie rivers. They fished in the river and gathered crayfish and fresh-water mussels; they traveled higher into the mountains to gather roots, nuts, and berries; they hunted mountain goat and deer; and from the base of the mountains at Snoqualmie Pass, they obtained a talc-like paint, which they used for barter, among other things.

The Yakimas lived just east of Snoqualmie Pass and southeastward another 100 miles to the Yakima River's confluence with the Columbia. Theirs was a plateau culture, the name of their tribe meaning "People of the Gap or Narrow Waters." Their main winter camp was located at what we now call Union Gap near Yakima. One of their tribal legends concerned a terrible battle between Speel-yi (Coyote God) and Wish-poosh (Big Beaver or Evil God), which made the channel of the Yakima River and tore gaps in the ridges downstream.

There were several divisions of Yakima Indians. One group had a winter camp in the Kittitas Valley, and others were scattered up and down the greater Yakima Valley. The Kittitas–Cle Elum group of Yakimas had villages along the upper Yakima near Thrall, at the head of Yakima Canyon; near Ellensburg, west of Thorp; and on the Yakima River where it is joined by the Swauk and by the Teanaway. When white exploration began in the mid-1800s, the Cle Elum group lived year 'round at the foot of Lake Cle Elum. From spring through fall, the village occupants fanned out to summer camps not far below the snowline.

The Yakimas spoke the Shahaptian lingual type. They and the Snoqualmies seem to have spent a great deal of time in each other's camps, trading and intermarrying. The Kittitas group had an especially active trade with the Snoqualmies on the west side of the Cascades. On several occasions, white explorers saw members of the Yakimas wintering with the Snoqualmie Indians in the Tokul Creek village, below Snoqualmie Falls.

As soon as spring arrived, the large camps of Yakimas split up into family groups and set out to gather roots and bulbs as they moved upward into the mountains. When autumn turned the mountain larch a flaming gold, they returned to their base villages. After digging wild onion and the bulbs of camas and kouse plants and preparing them for winter by baking, drying, or pulverizing, they moved on for nuts and huckleberries. As the Snoqualmies did, they probably practiced burning in certain areas of the forest to improve berry-picking grounds. Late in the fall they camped at the large fisheries at the outlets of Lakes Kachess and Cle Elum. Here, they built an elaborate system of weirs to concentrate the fish during the salmon runs into these lakes.

Around the 1740s, the horse arrived in the Northwest, introduced via other tribes who acquired them from the Spaniards. This must have enhanced long-distance travel for the Indians and increased trading trips through the mountains by way of the route through Yakima Pass. Camps established along the way at berry and fishing areas provided good opportunities for socializing and bartering.

Every few years Indians from all Northwest tribes gathered at a large camp in the Kittitas Valley, adjacent to the trail, to hold council talks, make peace, settle disputes, trade, socialize, and dig roots from high-producing grounds nearby. The gathering place was known as Che-ho-lan. There were ample springs of water nearby and the creeks carried their spring runoff to the Yakima River.

Indians converged by the thousands, coming from Puget Sound, central Washington and parts of what is now eastern Washington, Oregon, Idaho, and British Columbia. There were men, women, and children from a wide variety of cultural backgrounds. Early white observers, who came to barter for horses in 1814 and later in 1863, would never forget the sight of this great encampment. Alexander Ross in his book, *Canoe and Saddle*, and A. J. Splawn in *Kamiakin* both described the camp as very large. Ross thought it was six miles across and counted 3,000 Indians, exclusive of women and children.

While the women and children dug kouse and penua (sweet potato), the men rode off to hunt. At the same time, there were horse racing and stick bone playing. Chained bears and wolves added to the noise. There was also a great deal of trading going on.

What was being traded? Dentalium shell necklaces from the coast; shell and abalone money; shell adornment for ear and

Yakima Indian dwelling, about 1912.

nose wearing; copper bracelets; obsidian scrapers; arrowheads and other items from Oregon or British Columbia; hair from mountain goats and dogs for weaving blankets; bark and various roots for basket weaving; owl's-foot necklaces; antler chippers; ornately carved wood, stone, and bone implements; buffalo robes and blankets from the plains Indians, brought back by plateau Indians who had "gone to buffalo" the year before.

Near the camp, the east-west Snoqualmie Trail linked the western coast and the plains. The Indians were in much closer touch with each other than the white man realized then or now.

Left, *Pat Kanim, identified as a chief of the Snoqualmies in the 1850s.*

Below, *Ka-Mi-Akin, "The Last Hero of the Yakimas,"* 1900.

In the 1840s and 1850s, when the first white Americans began arriving in the area, the Indians on both sides of the Cascades had already been influenced by the European culture of the early explorers and fur traders. The population had been greatly reduced by smallpox and other epidemics of the white man's diseases, and the culture was being changed by the life styles and trappings of the white man. The area's first cattlemen on the bunch-grass plains east of the Cascades were Indian. In the early 1830s, the Hudson's Bay Company herded cattle north from California to raise beef for their stations and for export. Many were taken east of the Cascades to be raised by Indians, who then annually herded them back west through Naches Pass, south of Snoqualmie Pass, to the Hudson's Bay fort at Nisqually, at the southern end of Puget Sound.

It is not known which of the two routes over the mountains — Yakima Pass or Snoqualmie Pass — the Indians began using first, or if the initial use was simultaneous, but the passes seem to have been treated as a unit by the Indians. Early white explorers, searching for a possible wagon road over the Cascades, were hampered in their efforts before they recognized the distinction — the Indians used the foot trail over what the whites later called "the true Snoqualmie Pass." It followed the South Fork Snoqualmie River to the summit at Snoqualmie Pass and descended to Lake Keechelus. There they either used canoes to cross the lake or took a trail around the east side and over a spur of Keechelus Ridge to the south end of the lake. On the east side of Snoqualmie Pass — at the lower end of Lake Keechelus — another trail led south past Lost Lake and over Yakima Pass (also known as Cedar River Pass), then along the Cedar River, finally rejoining the first trail on the west end. Generally, the Indians used Snoqualmie Pass for foot traffic and the higher route over Yakima Pass for traveling on horseback. (The latter was less obstructed by downed timber and thick underbrush.)

When the whites came to explore the passes, the Indians guided them over Yakima Pass but told them of deep snows on Snoqualmie Pass. When the confusion was finally cleared and development of Snoqualmie Pass as a wagon route over the mountains began, the white men discovered the truth of the Indians' earlier description. It *was* a difficult route to build a road over, yet as the lowest crossing in that vicinity of the Cascades, it remained the most desirable.

2

Two Passes, Three Expeditions

The exit sign on I-90 for Tinkham Road and McClellan's Butte Trail, about ten miles west of the Cascade divide, bears the names of two explorers who attempted expeditions on the Snoqualmie Pass route in the 1850s. It is clear now, however, that for some twenty years there were two passes that the settlers referred to as "Snoqualmie Pass," and that the one actually explored by Abiel Tinkham and George McClellan was the old Indian horse trail, known today as Yakima Pass.

The explorations began in 1853, prompted by Congressional policies and the growing population on Puget Sound. By that year, the mountains had come to be recognized as a frustrating and troublesome bottleneck to transportation, trade, and regional growth. There were no roads through the mountains north of the Columbia River, and the Willamette Valley, south of the Columbia River, enticed most of the arriving wagonloads of immigrants, who could travel directly through the Cascades over Barlow Pass, south of Mount Hood. Pioneer travelers found it particularly inconvenient to get down the Columbia and up the Cowlitz rivers to Puget Sound because of the necessity of alternating boat and wagon travel. The Puget Sound pioneers hoped a direct-line wagon road could be built north from the Umatilla River to Fort Walla Walla on the Columbia River. (This fort—also known as Fort Nez Perce—was the original Fort Walla Walla and was located near where the town of Wallula is today. The old fort site is now underwater as the result of a dam. A new Fort Walla Walla was built in 1857 in the present-day town of Walla Walla.)

The idea behind a direct-line wagon road was to siphon wagon trains off the Oregon Trail directly through the Cascades across either Naches Pass or Snoqualmie Pass. From the Indians and Hudson's Bay people, the pioneers knew or suspected that wagon roads could be made of the ancient, well-trod Indian paths through the mountains, and by 1853 they were at work on a wagon road through Naches Pass, north of present-day Chinook Pass.

That same year, Congress authorized a large appropriation for four transcontinental railroad surveys across the western expanses of mountains and deserts, and one — the northern survey from the Great Lakes to Puget Sound — was begun. President Pierce appointed Isaac Stevens as first territorial governor of the newly formed Washington Territory and put him in charge of this northern survey, as well as of making treaties with the Indians.

Governor Stevens divided the survey, with one branch coming from St. Louis up the Missouri to the mouth of the Yellowstone, directed by Lieutenant Abiel Tinkham among others, and with another, directed by Governor Stevens himself, from the Great Lakes to Fort Colville in northeastern Washington. Stevens gave a second officer, Captain George McClellan, two important tasks: to find a railroad route through the Cascades and to assist the settlers in building a military road from Fort Steilacoom on Puget Sound to Fort Walla Walla through Naches Pass. Congress had just authorized $20,000 for this project.

Reports had reached Secretary of War Jefferson Davis that the snows of the Rockies and Cascades would be too much for running trains through in winter, and Stevens was especially interested in examining this theory. The surveys began in March; Congress was expecting them to be completed by the end of December, with full reports ready for the next session of Congress in 1854.

McClellan sailed from the East to the West Coast via the Isthmus of Panama and did not arrive in Washington Territory, at Fort Vancouver on the lower Columbia River, until late June 1853. It took a month to get his party organized before he set out with 65 men on horseback and 100 horses for packing supplies and scientific survey instruments.

Since the Columbia River still had high water from the spring runoff, he chose not to take the usual trail along the river to The

George B. McClellan

Dalles through the Cascades, but took an inland trail just south of Mount St. Helens. The party's scientific officers heard from the Indians that the mountain had erupted in 1842.

From the beginning, McClellan's efforts were plagued with problems. A rumor circulated ahead of his travels that his expedition was coming to seize the horses and cattle of the Yakimas and to take their country by force. It became very difficult for him to find Indian guides, which may partly explain why his large party moved only about four and one-half miles a day through the difficult terrain. They eventually made it through the Klickitat Indian country after providing gifts and taking pains to explain that this mission was not to harm the Yakimas.

By August 17, McClellan's party had reached the Ahtanum Mission on the Yakima River near Union Gap. This Catholic mission was a favorite stopping place for early-day explorers, as the priests knew much about the Indians and the country thereabouts. After obtaining food from the mission, McClellan's men located a depot camp in the Wenas Valley, and Chief Kamiakin of the Yakimas was invited in for formal talks. Working from the assumption that the Indian country was to become a thoroughfare for the white man, McClellan believed it was important to make a proper impression and establish a friendly understanding. He explained the workings of the white man's government and his intention of building a wagon road through the

Yakima country — the road that the pioneer settlers had begun over Naches Pass to connect Forts Steilacoom and Walla Walla.

He then conducted a scouting trip over Naches Pass from east to west and back again. He pronounced it impractical for a railroad and thought it a poor wagon route, not usable in winter. He also decided he did not have time to work on it as a military road, returned to the Wenas Valley, and headed north to explore Snoqualmie Pass. Although one wagon train did make it through Naches Pass that fall, it was a very difficult route and never became popular.

Traveling overland from the Wenas Valley to the Kittitas Valley, McClellan established another depot camp near a trail junction not far from the present site of Ellensburg. His next task was to investigate a route through Snoqualmie Pass. Although the Indians told McClellan that snow would be knee-deep at the mouth of the Yakima and would increase in depth all along the route until it reached a depth of twenty-five feet at the summit of the Cascades, McClellan continued.

With a party of nine men on horseback, he set out from the depot camp on September 4 and headed in the direction of Snoqualmie Pass. The route was along the Indian trail — now approximated by I-90 from exit 100 at the Thorp interchange over what is locally known as Thorp Prairie and dropping down Indian John Hill — to a prairie along the Yakima River, just east of Cle Elum. In exchange for three shirts, a dress, a cap, and other small items, an Indian who came into camp agreed to take him through the mountains over the Snoqualmie route. They pressed on and camped one more night on the trail, probably near Easton, before reaching the pass.

The party passed by Lake Keechelus and began their climb to what McClellan thought was Snoqualmie Pass, but was actually Yakima Pass. The trail was so steep that they had to lead their horses part of the way, along the ridge between Roaring and Meadow creeks west of Lake Keechelus.

They camped just below and east of Yakima Pass Tuesday night, September 6, 1853. The next day they rode to the summit, then sent the animals back to camp and walked about three miles west, down the steep trail into the Cedar River drainage. One man in the party as well as the guide felt the descent too steep for a wagon road, so they turned back to their last camp, taking compass bearings and barometric readings of the pass area. The guide told McClellan that the high rough mountains he saw to the north formed the dividing ridge between the Yakinse (Yakima) and the Sinahomis (Snoqualmie). The explorer reasoned that these mountains must be too high to consider making a route through them. To further frustrate explorations, the air was filled with dense smoke from forest fires, reducing visibility. McClellan, even as today's travelers, was thrown off by the geography of Snoqualmie Pass. As car travelers pass Lake Keechelus westbound on I-90, they actually are traveling north. At the summit, the highway swings around a sharp turn and heads south, then at the bottom of the grade west of the pass, the road finally swings to the west. In short, it is easy to get turned around at Snoqualmie Pass. (This is one reason the area is something of a graveyard for small planes; when clouds obscure the peaks and other landmarks, pilots following the road often forget it takes several turns.)

From his viewpoint 5 miles farther south and 500 feet higher in Yakima Pass, McClellan could not know of the route through the true Snoqualmie Pass—except that the Indian guide told him there was a route. McClellan could have explored that route, but apparently had had all the pass exploration he could take for the time being. In his summary of the area to Governor Stevens, McClellan did speak of a foot trail leading from the head of Lake Keechelus to the head of the South Fork Snoqualmie River. He explained that the Indians represented it as seldom used and practicable on foot with the greatest difficulty. He described it as passable only for an active, unencumbered man.

Though McClellan's visit to the area has been looked upon as a failure by many, he did gather basic information, which makes his notes interesting reading. For instance, he gives an almost step-by-step account of leading his horse up the Indian trail from Lake Keechelus to the summit of Yakima Pass and mentions specific landmarks that can still be seen today. He noticed that Lost Lake fluctuated each season and that it had a visible outlet only when it was full. The rest of the year, its outlet, known as Roaring Creek, sprang out of the rocks in an old stream channel about one-half mile down the canyon from the lake. This is still the situation today.

McClellan ran a barometric profile over Yakima Pass and noted that Lake Keechelus is the head of the Yakima River. He also noted that, as far as Lake Keechelus, a good road could be carved up the length of the Yakima River from its confluence with the Columbia, 100 miles east. He observed that the Indians fished in the mountain lakes and even carried canoes to Lost (Wilailootzas) Lake, where they caught trout.

McClellan's guide led the party on a slightly different trail back toward the depot camp in the lower Kittitas Valley, this time on the north side of the Yakima so they could visit the fisheries at Lakes Kachess and Cle Elum. It is too bad they did not attempt to follow the Indian footpath around the east side of Lake Keechelus and at least visit the true Snoqualmie Pass.

Between the time McClellan concluded his futile efforts, reached Olympia at the southern end of Puget Sound, by way of the Columbia Gorge, and made his report, Governor Stevens had also had time to reach Olympia and had talked with local pioneers. He got a truer picture of travel routes through the Cascades and decided to assign one of his engineers from the St. Louis–to–Rocky Mountain leg of his expedition to travel through Snoqualmie Pass in midwinter. Stevens did not believe the view of a twenty-five-foot snow depth on the crest of the Cascades, nor was he going to let McClellan off so easily.

Stevens sat down in Olympia and quickly penned a letter to Abiel Tinkham, a young engineer who had performed some outstanding exploits at fearlessly tackling three known crossings of the Rocky Mountains in late fall weather. Even now — if he survived the experience — Abiel Tinkham was crossing the southern Nez Perce Trail through the Bitterroot Mountains approaching Fort Walla Walla from the east. In mid-December, 1853, Stevens dispatched the letter by military express; it took two weeks for a rider on horseback to personally carry it down the Cowlitz River to Fort Vancouver, then up the Columbia and across the desert to Fort Walla Walla.

Coincidentally, the letter arrived just a day after Tinkham reached the fort. He had indeed had a harrowing mountain crossing, accompanied by three other white men and an Indian guide. They had sent their horses back to another camp on the other side of the mountains and on self-made snowshoes had made a brave crossing, traveling much of the way through six- and eight-foot snowdrifts. Equipped with only two blankets, a tin cup, and a change of moccasins and socks apiece, plus the clothes on their backs and flour and salt as food rations, they had struggled the better part of 100 miles to the winter camp of

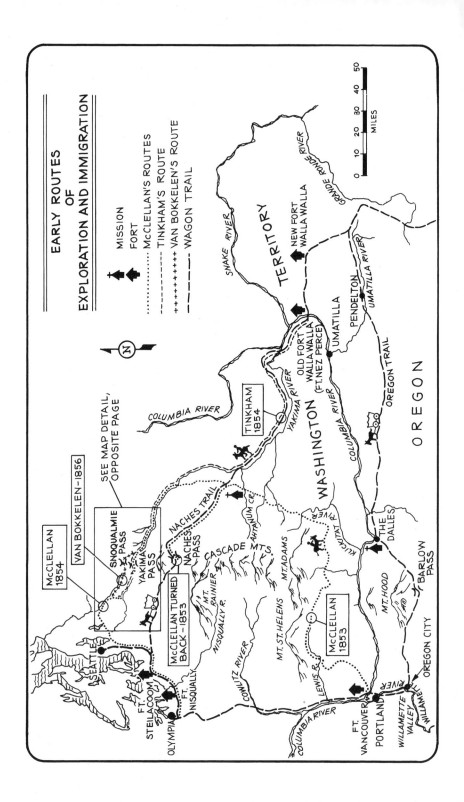

EARLY ROUTES
OF
EXPLORATION AND IMMIGRATION

MISSION
FORT
McCLELLAN'S ROUTES
TINKHAM'S ROUTE
VAN BOKKELEN'S ROUTE
WAGON TRAIL

MILES
0 10 20 30 40 50

TERRITORY

WASHINGTON

OREGON

COLUMBIA RIVER

SNAKE RIVER

GRANDE RONDE RIVER

NEW FORT
WALLA WALLA

UMATILLA RIVER

PENDELTON

UMATILLA

OLD FORT
WALLA WALLA
(FT. NEZ PERCE)

YAKIMA RIVER

COLUMBIA RIVER

OREGON TRAIL

THE DALLES

KLICKITAT RIVER

TINKHAM
1854

SEE MAP DETAIL,
OPPOSITE PAGE

VAN BOKKELEN-1856

McCLELLAN
1854

SNOQUALMIE
PASS

NACHES TRAIL

YAKIMA
PASS

NACHES
PASS

AHTANUM CR.

CASCADE MTS.

MT. ADAMS

MT.
RAINIER

MT. ST. HELENS

McCLELLAN TURNED
BACK - 1853

McCLELLAN
1853

SEATTLE

FT.
STEILACOOM

OLYMPIA

FT.
NISQUALLY

NISQUALLY R.

COWLITZ RIVER

LEWIS R.

MT. HOOD

BARLOW
PASS

FT.
VANCOUVER

PORTLAND

OREGON CITY

WILLAMETTE
VALLEY

WILLAMETTE RIVER

COLUMBIA RIVER

N

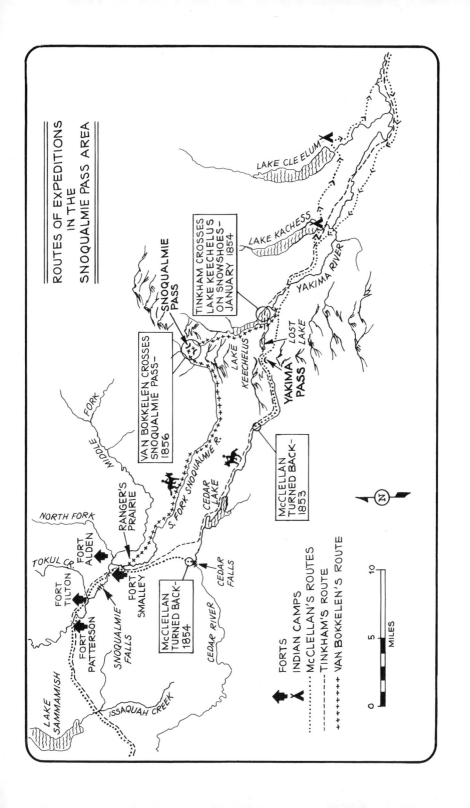

ROUTES OF EXPEDITIONS
IN THE
SNOQUALMIE PASS AREA

LAKE CLE ELUM

TINKHAM CROSSES
LAKE KEECHELUS
ON SNOWSHOES—
JANUARY 1854

LAKE KACHESS

YAKIMA RIVER

SNOQUALMIE
PASS

VAN BOKKELEN CROSSES
SNOQUALMIE PASS—
1856

LAKE
KEECHELUS

LOST
LAKE

YAKIMA
PASS

MIDDLE   FORK

RANGER'S
PRAIRIE

S. FORK SNOQUALMIE R.

CEDAR
LAKE

McCLELLAN
TURNED BACK—
1853

NORTH FORK

FORT
ALDEN

FORT
TILTON

TOKUL CR.

FORT
SMALLEY

McCLELLAN TURNED BACK—
1854

CEDAR
FALLS

FORT
PATTERSON

SNOQUALMIE
FALLS

CEDAR RIVER

LAKE
SAMMAMISH

ISSAQUAH CREEK

N

FORTS

INDIAN CAMPS

McCLELLAN'S ROUTES
....

TINKHAM'S ROUTE
- - - - -

VAN BOKKELEN'S ROUTE
+ + + + + +

0   5   10

MILES

the Nez Perce. Here, they had rested a week, obtained horses, and traveled west to the home of a white settler, where they had spent Christmas and obtained food supplies for the remainder of the 165-mile horseback ride to Walla Walla.

Stevens's letter arrived the day of New Year's Eve. Along with other residents of the fort, Tinkham saw the New Year in to the music of a fiddle and dancing. It must have been a merry celebration of both arriving and departing for the ambitious native of Maine, who was ready to set out to cross the Cascades at once, waiting only for new horses to arrive from The Dalles.

In his letter, Stevens rather apologetically asked Tinkham to take on the formidable task of a winter crossing of the Cascades right after his exhausting expedition through the Bitterroots. He told Tinkham the routes he should take to Olympia if the mountains proved too much and he had to backtrack. The governor also suggested what supplies to take and advised Tinkham to barter for four cattle from among the Walla Wallas and to herd them along the trail for meat.

The explorer, however, chose one horse from the Indians to use for his meat, as it would make better time being herded. He also chose to dismiss his white companions to give them a rest from the arduous task ahead, deciding to make the trip with Indians only. Where McClellan had problems in finding Indian guides, Tinkham had none. He had adapted to their life style and got along well with them.

The party forded the Columbia River by swimming across and started up the trail toward Snoqualmie Pass on January 7, 1854. Tinkham paid careful attention to the snow depths all along the way as his three Walla Walla Indian guides took him toward the winter village of the Yakimas near Union Gap, where he too would visit the Ahtanum Mission.

Simultaneously, Stevens sent McClellan from Olympia to explore the Snoqualmie route from the west. Not able to obtain horses, McClellan set out by canoe with a small party of white men and Indians and headed north toward the Snoqualmie River. They reached a camp where Tokul Creek enters the river, just below Snoqualmie Falls, on January 7. McClellan and his men walked around the falls and climbed a three-mile trail to cross the river once more in a smaller canoe, then walked across Ranger's Prairie — the site of present-day North Bend. Then the captain left his men behind and walked on a short way through the forest toward the site now known as Cedar Falls. He was headed once more, unwittingly, toward Yakima Pass. He had come ill equipped and was turned back by a few inches of snow on the trail. It was at this point that McClellan finally recognized that the pass he was headed toward was not Snoqualmie Pass. While walking along with the Indians, McClellan once more heard stories of deep snows in the mountains on the horse path leading to the Yakima Pass divide. Once more he neglected to check out the footpath through the true Snoqualmie Pass. By January 11, 1854, he was back on tidewater, heading north in his canoe to explore other areas.

In the meantime, Tinkham was making progress traveling from east to west into the mountains. His Walla Walla guides turned back after reaching the mission. The weather had, by now, turned bitterly cold; it was not the best time of year to be seeking Indian guides to cross the Cascades. Even with the help of the priests, it took him a couple of days to coax any Indians who knew the trail to leave their warm quarters. Eventually two Yakima Indians were found, and they continued with Tinkham on horseback to another Indian winter camp near Lake Cle Elum, not far from present-day Roslyn.

Though the weather was cold, the snow was not deep. Tinkham saw thousands of horses and some cattle wintering on the bunch-grass plains and hills all along the route from where the Yakima entered the Columbia, upstream to the lower Kittitas Valley. The dreamed-of wagon and railroad route through the region was so far not buried beneath the snow depths that McClellan had feared.

However, snow was about two feet deep in the area of Lake Cle Elum, and Tinkham realized that this was the end of the line for horseback travel. He sent one of the Yakimas back to the camp with instructions to return the horses to Fort Walla Walla. He arranged for four of the Indians from the Cle Elum area to accompany him, increasing the party to six. In his diary, later included in Stevens's report in 1854, Tinkham wrote, "Sending back my horses in the care of an Indian, to be returned to Wallah-Wallah, the balance of the exploration was conducted on foot, and with snow-shoes when necessary. To aid in packing, and also from the necessity of procuring an additional guide, I here increased my Indians to five in number. From them I obtained dried salmon, which they have in abundance, and a variety of dried roots."

He spent a night in their comfortable winter lodge before tackling the rest of the trip. Tinkham's previous experience packing on snowshoes had taught him to dispense with all items not absolutely essential to sustenance and health. He, therefore, traveled without a tent to make his equipment as light as possible.

On January 20, 1854, the party camped at the foot of Lake Keechelus. The explorer described the snow within twelve miles of the camp as having an average depth no greater than two and a half feet — a dry, cold snow. Farther on, he found that snow depth varied from four to six feet, and at the night camp was some four feet deep. He found the lakes frozen and covered with snow, and their smooth, even surfaces afforded easy traveling for snowshoes.

It snowed eighteen inches the night of his Lake Keechelus camp. He took an average measurement of the snow from Lake Keechelus to the summit and found it to be about six feet, frequently running as high as seven feet. The new snow was light and dry, and progress in it was slow and laborious. Tinkham felt, however, that these snows presented little obstruction to removal in comparison with the compact, drifted snows of the Atlantic states. He saw little barrier to train passage.

Traveling the five miles from Lake Keechelus to the summit of Yakima Pass, the party followed the ravine of Roaring Creek and snowshoed the length of Lost Lake, rather than taking the much steeper, parallel ridge route that McClellan had used in September. Tinkham noted that the snow remained six feet deep for only a dozen miles of the route; the level then dropped rapidly until the upper end of what the Indians called Nook-Noo Lake (Cedar Lake). Here they cached their snowshoes for the return trip. The Indians even told Tinkham the party might travel back through the mountains over the foot trail through Snoqualmie Pass in a month, and they expected less snow on that route. It took the party five days to travel from Lake Keechelus by way of Yakima Pass to the camp of the Snoqualmie Indians below Snoqualmie Falls. On January 27, 1854, Tinkham arrived at the little village on Elliott Bay known as Seattle. He traced a good line for a railroad down the Snoqualmie Valley to Seattle on his trip.

J. H. H. VanBokkelen

Tinkham and Stevens appeared in Washington, D.C., before Congress to vouch personally for the northern railroad survey, but their pleas to choose this route went ignored. Their work was not in vain, however, for the findings of Tinkham's winter trip and McClellan's explorations were the basis for future rail and road surveys through the mountains and for the development that finally came through the true Snoqualmie Pass.

The first recording of a government-backed, white American party to cross Snoqualmie Pass followed well over two years behind McClellan and Tinkham. During this period, marked by Indian wars, Snoqualmie Pass was seen as an important communication link between the Indians east and west of the mountains. Major J. H. H. Van Bokkelen of the Washington Territorial Volunteers was scouting the area for a location to build military fortifications against possible attack from eastern Washington Indians on the settlers of Puget Sound.

His task was aided by the presence of friendly Snoqualmie Chief Pat Kanim and over 100 of his warriors. Governor Stevens's orders were to watch and, if necessary, to blockade Snoqualmie and Yakima passes, and to send scouts over the mountains to explore and make topographical notes of the country — the distance and depth of snows, the locations of streams and foot trails, and descriptions of prairies and mountains. The Territorial Volunteers were to erect blockhouses on

the prairie above and below Snoqualmie Falls and make sketches
of the country. Some troops were also ordered to open new
roads and repair old ones from one defensive point to another.
In seeing to the defense of this thoroughfare, Van Bokkelen
supervised the construction of four military forts in the Snoqualmie River Valley area. Fort Tilton was the largest of these,
built in February, 1856, one mile below Snoqualmie Falls. It was
built of unpeeled hemlock logs, stood over six feet tall, and was
on a site where the soldiers could observe anyone going upstream or downstream. As many as 200 men were stationed
there at one time. Today, its location is indicated by a sign on
private land on Fish Hatchery Road along the Snoqualmie River.

By the time of Van Bokkelen's expedition, people had begun to
sort out which pass was which and were usually referring to
them correctly. While different forts were being built, Van Bokkelen and his men scouted the two passes. One party was sent
over Yakima Pass on horseback while Van Bokkelen and another
group backpacked along the Snoqualmie Pass Indian footpath.

From a letter Van Bokkelen penned while in a camp at
Snoqualmie Pass comes the best description of this epic mission:

Sir: In accordance with my last communication, the parties started
for this place by the different trails. I went with Capt. Beam and
his company by the foot trail from Ranger's prairie [now the site
of North Bend at the foot of Mount Si], sending the pack train
with Company I and H by the horse trail on Cedar Creek. After
traveling a mile through the bottom I came into prairie of fine
grass, about two and one-half miles long and three-fourths wide.
After leaving the prairie I went through the timber for a mile and
struck a burnt prairie with rock soil about three miles long, after
leaving which I commenced a gradual rise to the summit of the
pass, which thirty five miles from Ranger's prairie the whole trail
is a gradual rise, but greatly obstructed with timber and would re-
quire considerable labor to open. After raising the summit [of
Snoqualmie Pass] we lost the old Indian trail, and I took a road
with a gradual slope to the south, with the intention of striking
Cichelass [Keechelus] Lake, which I struck after traveling fourteen
miles. About four miles before I struck the lake I found an Indian
trail which I followed to within one hundred yards of the lake,
where I found blazes on the trees to the lake which appeared to
have been made by white men; commencing from the lake they
must have gone that far and returned, giving it up as a bad job. I
should like to know if a white man has ever been through before

we went through this time, for we could find no signs of white men on the road. The trail at this place runs into the lake, and the Indians in using this trail must either cross the lake in canoes or travel around the shores of the lake in the dry season. From this place we took the western side of the lake and forced our way along over rocks and timber, up hill and down, for eight miles, till we got to the lower end of the lake, when we struck the pack trail where we camped.

A look through Van Bokkelen's reports brings some other things to light. He forgot to mention that three Indians were found watching his overnight encampment at Snoqualmie Pass and an unsuccessful pursuit of them followed. (This was later indicated in another report.) While the major waited at the foot of Lake Keechelus, he sent a small party of men down the Yakima River to scout farther east. They found a fresh Indian encampment, with fish traps in the river but no Indians. These men felt that a fort would be wise at a point on the Yakima about twenty miles downstream from Lake Keechelus. The horses that Van Bokkelen had requested from the quartermaster at Olympia did not come, however, so he had to fall back to his defense posts in the Snoqualmie River Valley. Besides Fort Tilton, there were by now three other forts — Fort Alden, where Meadow-brook is now; Fort Smalley on Tollgate Farm, just across the bridge from North Bend on the Snoqualmie–Fall City Road; and Fort Patterson, located about where Fall City is now.

The members of the battalion built a road around Snoqualmie Falls in order to supply their forts. Van Bokkelen's report states "...in all our movements we have gone through an entirely wild country, and have been compelled to open our own roads and build roads, and not have it done for us as other battalions have...."

When the hostilities were over and there was no longer any threat of Indian attack via Snoqualmie Pass, the volunteers who served in Van Bokkelen's battalion could leave, but several stayed on in the Snoqualmie Valley to try living the settler's frontier life. Several forts were no longer needed for defensive purposes and were converted to farms. By the 1860s, when the first handful of settlers found their way into the Snoqualmie Valley, the former military men were drifting out, possibly driven out by the loneliness of the deep forests. By now, all traces of the old forts have disappeared.

3

The Early Road

It is hard to imagine today a time when the federal and state governments did not have the funds to support a project considered as vital as the Snoqualmie Wagon Road. In the 19th century, the federal government built only military roads and there were a number in Washington Territory. However, the government did not see Snoqualmie Pass as a necessary military route as the Columbia River route was easier. The early building and maintenance of the Snoqualmie Wagon Road fell on the shoulders of local people, county governments, and small private companies that saw the great need for the completion of the missing link in east-west transportation.

By the summer of 1855, Seattle-area settlers, recognizing the potential boon to local economy, had caught the enthusiasm for a wagon road through the pass. A party of local men set out on a surveying trip. They, too, mistook Yakima Pass for the lowest route through the mountains. Even though soon afterwards the passes began to be distinguished from each other, the road across was long in coming. Because of the Indian wars — not to mention the formidable barrier the mountains presented to the manpower and tools available — it was another ten years before a second survey party's efforts resulted in the beginning of work on an actual road through the true Snoqualmie Pass.

From around 1858, however, the trail saw increasing traffic going on foot and horse to the mines of the Colville region. Tons of equipment and goods were shipped from Seattle over the trail on the backs of horses, mules, and men to the mines. It was reported that the trail was in such good condition that a healthy horse or mule could pack up to 250 pounds. In 1859, the territorial legislature of Washington sent a request to Congress for funds to build a wagon road from Seattle through the pass. However, the attention of Congress was focused on the problems between the North and the South, and the request got no further than the introduction of a bill in 1861. It would have provided $75,000 to build a military road from Walla Walla to Seattle.

In 1865, another party of Seattle men — A. A. Denny, L. V. Wykoff, John Ross, and William Perkins — explored Snoqualmie Pass with an eye to building a road. They rendezvoused at the lower end of Lake Keechelus with another party that had gone over Yakima Pass. While they were gone, Seattle residents raised over $2,500, and when the survey party returned, the first wagon road construction was begun from Ranger's Prairie (now North Bend) over the summit. William Perkins was awarded the roadwork contract; he worked with a force of twenty men from a camp set up at Ranger's Prairie. He and his men built twenty-five miles of the route over the most difficult part. It was left to local communities to build their own connecting roads. Even before Perkins and his men finished their work, a train of six wagons came over Snoqualmie Pass from the east, which meant that the travelers had built their own road as they went. These were the first wagons to come through the pass.

Though the road was now passable to wagon traffic, it was by no means an easy route to travel. For the first forty or so years of travel by wheeled vehicles through Snoqualmie Pass, water navigation across Lake Keechelus was a part of the mountain crossing. Tillman Houser, the first settler to come into the Kittitas Valley from Puget Sound, found that he could save quite a bit of time and backbreaking effort by building a raft to float his wagon, family, and livestock across. Rafting became an established practice for many years, except when lake waters lowered enough during dry spells to allow wagons to pass along the lake edge in shallow depths.

At one time, Flanagan Lumber Company, which had a mill on Lake Keechelus, had a barge on the lake for its own use. Before 1912, when Sidney Finch came to the lake from the Puget Sound area to run a ferry, men at the mill ran one on an irregular basis. Apparently, 1912 was the first year there was a regular ferry across Lake Keechelus.

For the early settlers, pushing the road through was only the

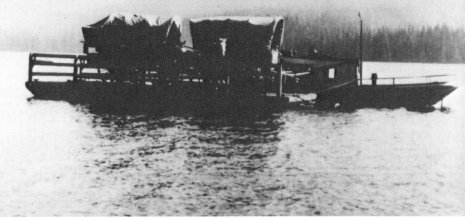

The ferry Wakiakum *on Lake Keechelus, operated by Sidney Finch, took covered wagons across.*

beginning of years of hard work, repairs, disappointments, and frustrations. The work was done with the most basic of tools and hand labor, and almost every year the job of reopening the route after a winter of rain, heavy snows, and spring runoffs fell to the first spring traveler wishing to cross the pass and meant almost as much work as the original clearing operation. For these travelers there were no emergency services as we know them today. If a wheel came off a wagon and could not be repaired, the immigrants had to remove what goods they could carry on their backs and horses and continue on foot to the nearest settlement in hopes of obtaining aid. As on the Oregon Trail, abandoned supplies often marked the route. There were numerous cases of immigrants turning back because of accidents, illness, or breakdowns.

The King County Commissioners had the Snoqualmie Wagon Road surveyed for the county in 1866. In May, they recommended that orders be drawn on the county treasurer for costs of surveying a route for a wagon road from the Black River bridge to Snoqualmie Pass. They further ordered the extension of the county road running from Black River bridge in the vicinity of present-day Renton to Ranger's Prairie. This road was now to travel through Snoqualmie Pass to the limits of King County.

Momentum was building, and the people of the county voted in favor of appropriating county funds for the project, 119 for, 4 against. In November, 1866, the commissioners ordered an appropriation of $2,500 to be spent on the road, and the territorial legislature subsequently voted another $2,000 on the condition that King County raise a like amount. Local residents worked

Automobile Club of Washington

To continue west to the pass, cars crossed the Columbia River at Vantage on this "Kitty-Grant" ferry.

hard, finding financial support in King County and elsewhere. Work continued on the road and it was finally fit for travel from Seattle to Ellensburg; in September, 1867, two men traveled through the pass from Umatilla to Seattle in only four days. The usual crossing took seven to fourteen days.

Nowadays, if we consider the question at all, we tend to think of much traffic over the pass as originating in Seattle, eastbound with foodstuffs and other goods for the smaller cities east of the Cascades. In the early days of the Snoqualmie Wagon Road, much of the traffic flow was westbound. It was a generally touted fact around Puget Sound that immigrants could save 500 miles by leaving the Oregon Trail and heading for Snoqualmie Pass, rather than following the circuitous route to Puget Sound via Portland and north up the Cowlitz River. Thanks to its advantageous location on the lower end of the Columbia River, Portland had been the Northwest center of commerce ever since settlers had begun to arrive. Ranchers east of the Cascades in Washington Territory were sending most of their livestock and grain trade down the Columbia River to Portland because that route offered the best market.

The opening of the Snoqualmie Wagon Road changed the whole perspective. Stockmen, tired of the exorbitant prices they were paying for shipping by steamship to Portland, discovered they had a ready market at a fraction of the transportation costs if they trailed their cattle through Snoqualmie Pass. In 1869, the cattle drives began. Ranchers began to funnel their cattle over the pass from what is now eastern and southern Idaho and from the northeast Oregon Territory — not to mention the Kittitas and

Yakima valleys. The drives launched the meat-packing industry in Seattle, which became a major West Coast meat-shipping point.

Train routes often followed wagon roads, and sure enough, surveyors for the Northern Pacific Railroad appeared at Snoqualmie Pass in 1867. The territorial legislature appropriated another $2,500 for work on the road in January, 1868, which was followed by the exciting news that the chief engineer for the Northern Pacific Railroad had decided Snoqualmie Pass was the favored route, and that Seattle would be the terminus of the railroad. Ultimately, the railroad went to Tacoma instead via Stampede Pass southeast of Snoqualmie Pass, but for the moment, the excitement prompted more work on the road. The appropriated funds went for new construction, repairs to the roadbed in the pass, and bridge building between Seattle and Ranger's Prairie, under the supervision of J. W. Borst.

The first plan for a private road company was promoted in the fall of 1869. Daniel Bagley, G. F. Whitworth, A. N. Merrick, H. A. Atkins, W. A. Shoudy, and C. P. Stone incorporated the Puget Sound Wagon Road Company, capitalized at $100,000. They planned to build a toll road over Snoqualmie Pass from Seattle to White Bluff on the Columbia River to connect with the head of steamship navigation, but their plan never got off the ground.

The Snoqualmie Wagon Road suffered a severe setback with the late fall rains and early spring snow runoff of 1869-70, rendering it virtually impassable to wagon traffic until late 1883 when the roadwork was completed in rough form. The only recorded crossing of the pass by wagons in those years was by John Shoudy, who crossed with two wagons in 1871 to buy supplies for his trading post east of the mountains; he and William Fawcett built the road as they went. The next year, he sent packtrains over the mountains instead. There were numerous attempts to rebuild the wagon road through these years, but the mountains remained nearly impassable by any wheeled traffic on a regular basis. As Congress continued to ignore the Washington Legislature's petitions for funds for a Snoqualmie Pass wagon route, the residents of Seattle, in 1875, came up with a plan to finance the project through several lotteries offering chances on downtown Seattle real estate. Some "prizes" turned out to be fake, but a genuine and unusual one was Henry Yesler's sawmill on the

Seattle waterfront, valued at $100,000. Complaints about some of the lottery promotion resulted in legal suits, and the courts declared the plans illegal before any drawings were held.

In the meantime, Kittitas Valley farmers had learned to farm using water from streams for irrigation, and the semi-desert lands were producing hay and grain crops as never before. Flour mills sprang up, and soon there were more mills in the Kittitas Valley producing finely ground grains than there were in all of the Puget Sound area. In addition to the cattle, sheep, horse, and swine drives headed west over the pass, there were frequent trips by packtrains bearing flour bound for Seattle. Supplies flowed by horse, mule, and human packer both east and west. It seems the people on both sides of the mountains were obsessed with moving large tonnages of supplies through, despite the nearly non-existent road.

During the winter of 1870-71, the Northern Pacific stationed two men in Snoqualmie Pass to make weather observations every six hours. This fact aroused new interest in the wagon road, which would be needed to supply railroad construction camps. In 1873, however, it was announced that Tacoma, rather than Seattle, would be the Puget Sound terminus for the Northern Pacific, by way of a newly discovered pass, later named Stam-

Cattle roundups were common in the Kittitas Valley around the turn of the century.
Oregon Historical Society

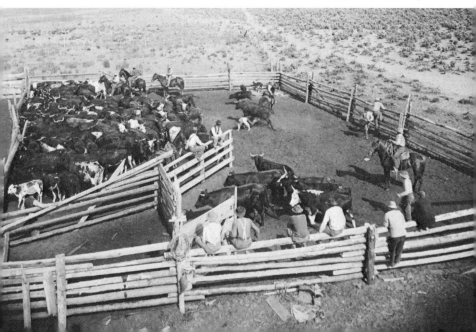

Above, log drives took place on the Yakima River, on the "flats" between Lake Keechelus and Cle Elum, about 1912. Below, river-logging camps had to be portable.

pede. Not to be daunted, local civic leaders proposed a Seattle and Walla Walla Railroad and Transportation Company, which would build a railroad over Snoqualmie Pass. The farthest east the line ever reached, however, was the coal mines near Renton. During this period, gold was discovered on Swauk Creek and slightly later on Peshastin Creek, both just east of the mountains. Miners rushed over Snoqualmie Pass to the mining camps, and claims were prospected on Swauk Creek and its tributaries. All the traffic to the mining camps helped keep alive the dream of a real road connecting east and west, and there were indications that such a road would also provide better access to the vast cedar forests on the west side.

By 1883, times were good in the territory. Ellensburg had become headquarters for supplying the mining camps of the Swauk-Blewett and Colville-Okanogan areas, as well as for settlers coming into the area. Ellensburg was also the county seat for all of what is now Kittitas and Chelan counties. What had been just a cow camp fifteen years earlier was now the hub of mining and ranching in the region, and it would soon be an important point on the approaching Northern Pacific Railroad. Sawmills at the headwaters of the Yakima River near the present town of Easton were sending logs down river to make railroad ties and build the bridge over the Columbia.

That same year, another proposal for a toll road across Snoqualmie Pass was introduced; this time it came from cattle interests in the Kittitas Valley. In March, 1883, a certificate of incorporation of the Seattle and Walla Walla Trail and Wagon Road Company was filed in Ellensburg. Officers were Walter Bull, president; George Smith, secretary; and Howard Walters, public relations agent. According to the company's statement of incorporation, it was formed "for the purpose of connecting Eastern and Western Washington Territory by means of trails and wagon roads through the Cascade mountains via the Snoqualmie Pass...." The company intended to construct, maintain, and operate the road, as well as purchase, lease, and sell or dispose of roads, trails, bridges, and ferries throughout the territory where necessary.

Employing the common tool of the day for informing the populace of any new plan or idea, Walters wrote squibs — favorable articles concerning the proposed wagon road project — for editors and publishers of newspapers on both sides of the Cas-

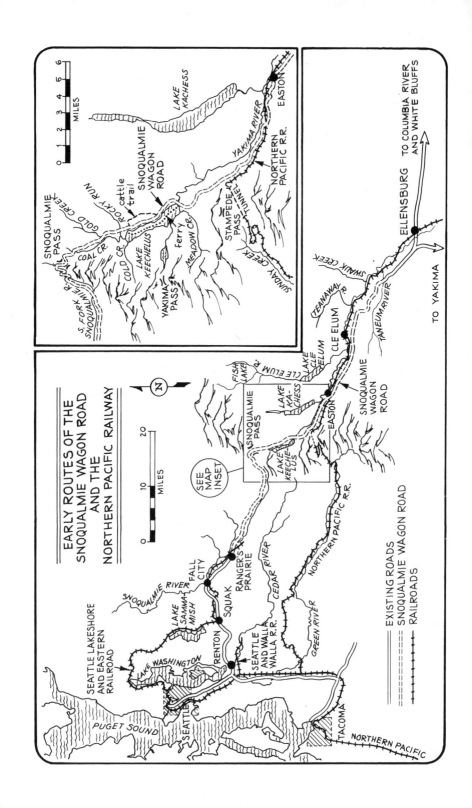

EARLY ROUTES OF THE
SNOQUALMIE WAGON ROAD
AND THE
NORTHERN PACIFIC RAILWAY

MILES
0   10   20

N

SEE MAP INSET

EXISTING ROADS
SNOQUALMIE WAGON ROAD
RAILROADS

MILES
0 1 2 3 4 5 6

SNOQUALMIE PASS

GOLD CREEK

COAL CR.

ROCKY RUN

COLD CR.

cattle trail

SNOQUALMIE WAGON ROAD

LAKE KEECHELUS

ferry

YAKIMA PASS

MEADOW CR.

S. FORK SNOQUALMIE R.

SUNDAY CREEK

STAMPEDE PASS TUNNEL

YAKIMA RIVER

NORTHERN PACIFIC R.R.

LAKE KACHESS

EASTON

TO COLUMBIA RIVER
AND WHITE BLUFFS

ELLENSBURG

TO YAKIMA

SWAUK CREEK

TEANAWAY R.

TANEUM RIVER

CLE ELUM

LAKE CLE ELUM

CLE ELUM RIVER

LAKE KACHESS

LAKE KEECHELUS

EASTON

SNOQUALMIE WAGON ROAD

SNOQUALMIE PASS

FISH LAKE

NORTHERN PACIFIC R.R.

FALL CITY

SNOQUALMIE RIVER

LAKE SAMMAMISH

SQUAK

RANGER'S PRAIRIE

CEDAR RIVER

RENTON

SEATTLE AND WALLA WALLA R.R.

GREEN RIVER

SEATTLE LAKESHORE AND EASTERN RAILROAD

LAKE WASHINGTON

SEATTLE

PUGET SOUND

TACOMA

NORTHERN PACIFIC

Certificate of $50 toll coupons for the Seattle and Walla Walla Trail and Wagon Road Co., 1883.

cades. Both Walters and Smith traveled to communities on either side of the pass that stood to benefit from the route and talked to anyone who might donate funds.

The funds began to come in — from Walla Walla, Ellensburg, and Seattle. Besides money, there were other donations, such as labor. Crews worked toward the summit of Snoqualmie Pass from both sides of the mountains during the summer. The road was projected to open to general travel over the pass on October 1, 1883, and at an earlier date for light immigrant travel.

By July, 1883, the road was passable for forty miles from the Taneum Bridge, southwest of Ellensburg, where the toll road began, to near Lake Keechelus. A crew of twenty men worked at bridging creeks, corduroying swamps, and making a good road as they moved west. Bridging the Yakima River was estimated to cost from $1,200 to $1,500; the road would cost $150 per mile, except for the corduroy part, which would cost $300 per mile. To check on construction, Smith took a herd of cattle to Seattle, and on his return trip he provided pack horses and saddles to anyone willing to make the crossing on the existing trail and completed sections of the road.

The article in the *Post-Intelligencer* further explained that when the road was completed, there would be "a stage line and mail route connecting Seattle with the east." The toll road would have "cabins and stables constructed not more than five miles apart along the snowy portion of the road."

When the road on the east side reached Lake Keechelus, a bridge was built along the north tip of the lake to avoid snow slides from the north and to eliminate the necessity of building

Miners heading for the ore fields of Gold Creek about 1898.

snowsheds. A large store was erected on either side of the pass to be used as company headquarters, with toll gates placed nearby.

The company succeeded in building the wagon road from Taneum Creek to Ranger's Prairie (now North Bend), and in August, 1884, the commissioners of Kittitas County authorized the company to collect the following tolls: for sheep or hogs, 10 cents per head; for loose cattle, horses, mules, or asses, 33⅓ cents per head; for a pack horse, 50 cents; for a man on horseback, $1; for one horse and buggy or other vehicle, $2; for two horses and buggy or wagon or other vehicle, $3; for four horses and wagon or other vehicle, $4. There is evidence that tolls were charged through 1887 and that the road continued to be used afterward, but in 1888 the Northern Pacific Railroad was completed across Stampede Pass to Tacoma. Traffic was accordingly diverted and the wagon road became less important to commerce.

In yet another burst of do-it-yourself-ism, at about the same time that the Ellensburg cattlemen were forming the Seattle and Walla Walla Trail and Wagon Road Company, a group of Seattle citizens again proposed to build a railroad of their own over Snoqualmie Pass. This time, the railroad was called the Seattle, Lake Shore and Eastern Railway Company. It was built as far as Squak (present-day Issaquah) in 1888 and extended as far east as Sallal Prairie (present-day Ken's Truck Town) in 1889.

During the 1880s and 1890s, both sides of the Cascades experienced a boom period. Coal was discovered just east of the Cascades, and Cle Elum and Roslyn were platted. Another town, by the name of Teanaway City, was platted with a view to its becoming an important rail center on the Northern Pacific, but it existed only two years or so. There was a mining boom north of Roslyn in the Fish Lake-Cle Elum River Valley, and regular horse-drawn stages met the Northern Pacific train in Cle Elum to carry goods and people back and forth to those mines. The coming of the railroad through Stampede Pass to Tacoma had drawn traffic away from Snoqualmie Pass, and by the late 1880s the road over Snoqualmie Pass was falling into disuse. Although still used by individuals during this boom period, the road was given no official maintenance.

In 1898, however, Seattle became the jumping-off point for the Klondike as the gold stampede began, and people poured into town by any transportation available. Several Kittitas Valley ranchers rented out their holdings and headed for Alaska; they and others who failed to strike it rich returned, prospecting their way east over the Snoqualmie Pass Wagon Road. Local papers were liberally sprinkled with news of the returning argonauts and of gold found in every stream across the mountains. Mining flourished on Gold Creek just north of Lake Keechelus, and the Flanagan Mining Company constructed a tramway-trestle that ran out of Gold Creek and Coal Creek and crossed over the wagon road.

In an April 3, 1899, article titled "Famous Lost Wagon Road," the *Seattle Post-Intelligencer* stated: "The coming summer will witness an attempt to revive the usefulness of the neglected and almost forgotten Snoqualmie Pass wagon road, once the great thoroughfare between Eastern and Western Washington. The legislature passed an act to provide $1000 for the improvement on the wagon road on condition that the two counties jointly raise a like amount. King shall contribute $700 and Kittitas County, $300 — the former benefitting more largely from the improvement if made." There must have been a certain amount of hyperbole attached to the article. The task fell under the supervision of David Denny, whose records of the summer show considerable traffic for a "lost" road. His report, preserved in the Washington State Library, also shows what it took to improve the road:

> Hon. Board of County Commissioners of King County, I herewith hand you my statement of labor performed, and money, provisions and tools received in the improvement of the Snoqualmie Pass Road.

I began work on the third day of June, 1899, and closed on the 23rd day of September. I made 412 feet of bridges and put down over 1200 feet of corduroy, made 3040 feet of new road and removed a large amount of rock from the road, nearly 200 blasts.

I commenced work on the left side or rather bank of the Yakima River, or outlet of Lake Kichelos, in Kittitas County. Around the shore of the lake I had great amount of rock work to do, there being many dangerous places in the road. In fact, it took just a month to complete the work around the lake. Then a half mile west of the lake the old road around Rocky Run was exceedingly bad, to avoid which I made a cut off of 1850 feet, made a 75 foot bridge and a good ford over the east branch of the creek. Just west of the 4 mile tree, I made two bridges and put down a quantity of corduroy, then a 40 foot bridge, all in the valley of Gold Creek. The crossing of Gold Creek in high water is dangerous and in fact impossible in extreme high water. I did all I could to improve the ford by shooting two logs which were in the water near the west bank. Just west of the crossing I made more corduroy and improved the crossing of an old channel of Gold Creek, then ½ mile west made another bridge, then rock work to the summit, the dividing line between the two counties, and from the west side to the first crossing of the South Fork of the Snoqualmie River. There I found the river was cutting the road away, and from every appearance one more winter and the road would be destroyed.

Spur rail lines were built to aid in construction of the Lake Keechelus dam.

U.S. Bureau of Reclamation, Yakima

David Denny, supervisor of Snoqualmie Pass wagon road repair in 1899, from south of Lake Keechelus to east of North Bend.

The report proceeds, describing how the crew relocated and rebuilt the road where possible to avoid two bad crossings of the Snoqualmie River:

> Then proceeding along west from the middle crossing the work was mainly removing rock until I reached what is known as the "Hump-backed Bridge," which I repaired and made a new bridge 75 feet long across the west branch of the same creek; then more rock work and corduroy until I reached the small creek just east of the 15 mile bridge. I made a 55 foot bridge over this creek and replaced the corduroy between the two bridges; I found a good ford a short distance above the bridge which can be used anytime when it is possible to use the road, and would recommend that it be put in shape to be used in case of any accident to the bridge.
>
> Coming west one mile, I found a long piece of road where the mud was very deep and getting deeper by the constant travel. So I made camp and put down nearly 1,000 feet of corduroy. Then moved camp to the Baxter Cabin just west of the 16 mile tree. Then I finished up by taking the stones out of the two long hills west of the cabin and some of the largest and worst of the boulders at the top of Grouse Ridge [near present-day Ken's Truck Town], and would have taken more out but that the constant

Camping in woods near Lake Keechelus, 1912.

rains had made it impossible to keep the powder dry, and consequently it would not work well. Speaking of the rain, I would say that it was a great hindrance to the work, causing the loss of several days.

In conclusion, I would most earnestly recommend the change of the road so as to avoid the two upper crossings of the river and a change of the road on Salale prairie [at the foot of Grouse Ridge] so as to avoid Grouse Ridge. The proper route would be to follow the middle fork road for a distance and then make side hill grade and strike the road near Grindstone Creek, making about one and one half miles of new road and saving as much in distance and avoiding the long pull up Perkins Back Bone or Grouse Ridge, as now called.

As to travel, I kept tally while on the road and found that from the time travel commenced until I closed work 94 wagons and carriages had passed over the road, 1148 horses had crossed the mountains, and the travel has continued unabated up to the present time, so that nearly two hundred wagons have crossed. People came in their covered wagons from Michigan and many points east. I estimate fully 19/20 of those crossing come to make homes in the Puget Sound valley, and that of itself is sufficient incentive to people on the west side to make a united effort to put the road in first class shape. Of course you understand that with $2000 less tools and provisions, I could only strike the worst places in 27 miles of mountain road! The sum should be ten times as much and then we could have a road in fair condition.

I find that the labor in Kittitas County amounted to about seven hundred and fifty nine dollars and that performed in King County to six hundred and forty five dollars. Not but what the road in King County needed more work to put it in a passable condition, but there were more dangerous places on the road in Kittitas County than there were in King County, and I felt it my first duty to make the road safe to life and limb, regardless of which county the work might have to be done in to put it in a safe condition. Furthermore I was laboring under the belief that the State appropriation was for the Snoqualmie Pass Road and not for any particular county.

Respectfully submitted,
D. Denny

Without fanfare, motorized traffic first went through Snoqualmie Pass in 1905, when Bert Harrison and a partner drove an 1898 Fryer-Miller automobile from Indianapolis to Seattle. According to Bert Harrison, Jr., they had to search from farm to farm for the main highway all through western Montana and

The old wagon road near Lake Keechelus, about 1915.

U.S. Bureau of Reclamation, Yakima

struggled against switchbacks and car trouble for two days from the Kittitas Valley to the Snoqualmie Summit. That same summer, Charles L. Ray and John Kelleher of Ellensburg drove a high-power Winton over the pass during the week of July 12. The most trouble they reported was in going around Lake Keechelus, where they were bothered by rocks and stumps. They had to jack up their machine several times to remove barriers. The two men camped out along the route.

Nothing more is said of cars crossing the pass until 1909, when the Alaska-Yukon-Pacific (AYP) Exposition was being held in Seattle. When it was learned that a transcontinental car race was planned from New York to Seattle in connection with the exposition, King, Kittitas, Yakima, and Walla Walla county commissioners quickly appropriated funds to improve the wagon road through their counties and over the summit.

The famed Pathfinder auto, which had recently won the New York-to-Paris race, started out from New York in March to go over the race route to Seattle. There was so much local excitement that a delegation of the few car owners living in Ellensburg drove out on the Wenas — a steep, desert road between Ellensburg and North Yakima (present-day Yakima) — to escort the Pathfinder to town. The Milwaukee Railroad had completed a line over Snoqualmie Pass from Ellensburg to Seattle that same year, and because the road over the summit was still so rough and primitive, the Pathfinder was ferried from Ellensburg over the mountains on a railroad flatcar.

It was originally believed that thirty-five or more cars would enter the race, but as word of the difficulty of the route got out, would-be entrants began to have second thoughts. On the day of the start, June 1 at 3:00 p.m., only six cars — an Itala, a Shawmut, an Acme, two Model T Fords, and a Stearns — began from New York's City Hall. President Taft's touch on a golden key simultaneously opened the car race and the Alaska-Yukon-Pacific Exposition in Seattle.

From St. Louis across the Midwest it might well have been called the Great Mud Race, for that was where the real competition began. There was a deluge of rain across Kansas and Wyoming, and after Granger, Wyoming, the racers were on their own, other transcontinental drivers having turned toward California at that point. Because they were in unmapped territory, the drivers hired men to pilot them through the maze of back-

Automobile Club of Washington

Snoqualmie Pass, July 1, 1916.

country roads. In southeastern Washington, one of the Fords got lost in the Horse Heaven Hills, causing the driver to fall behind while traveling eight miles along a railroad spur to get out of the desert. Somewhere in that area, someone struck a match on the side of the gas tank of the other Ford while it was refueling; no one was hurt badly, but the resulting fire destroyed fifteen gallons of precious gasoline, damaged the car, and sprang a leak in the tank, which caused problems for the rest of the trip.

Despite the fortitude they had shown in dealing with these and other hazards, the drivers looked ahead to Snoqualmie Pass with dread. In a pamphlet from the Ford Motor Company Archives called "The Race," one of the drivers wrote, "For weeks before the race we had been regaled with items concerning Snoqualmie Pass, the final stage of the journey. Report had it that perpetual snow lay deep on the roadway, snow from five to fifty feet in depth, snow that no automobile had ever surmounted. They told us how the Thomas Sixty Pathfinder had crossed on a flat car.... We were almost as scared of that pass as must have been some of those entrants who failed to start." Indeed, at best the road approaching Snoqualmie Pass from Ellensburg was only a single lane of dirt, bedrock, and gravel. Over the pass, it was worse, sometimes following the bed of the Snoqualmie River and never being more than a narrow, crude wagon passage.

On Tuesday, June 22, Ford No. 2 arrived in Ellensburg at 8:00 a.m. and pulled up at the Antlers Hotel. The Shawmut arrived fifteen minutes behind the Ford and stayed in Ellensburg just eight minutes before taking off. Ford No. 1 arrived a day later, and its crossing of Snoqualmie Pass is described in "The Race":

> We of Ford No. 1 were pushing on with the hope that here we would again overtake our up to that time luckier competitors. Ford No. 2 was reported stuck in the pass, the Shawmut was said to be in the ditch. But it was not so. Just before we started the ascent we learned of [Ford No. 2's] safe and triumphal arrival in Seattle — at the summit we got word of the Shawmut's getting in.
>
> We were on the top of the last difficulty. We had pushed through the snow with less trouble than we had expected. We would be in Seattle by four o'clock. When a rock hidden in the mud and snow sprang up to give us one last foul blow. For seven hours we worked on the top of the mountain up among the clouds remedying the trouble that rock had caused. At 5 p.m. we were going again. A half mile over the ties of the new "Milwaukee" railroad brought us to the down grade and ninety miles from the finish. The rest was easy.

The Acme arrived in Seattle a week later and the Itala followed on a freight car. The Stearns had never left New York State. Ford No. 2 was proclaimed winner of the $3,500 Guggenheim Trophy, although the win was apparently later declared illegal because the Ford had switched engines on the way. The Shawmut was then declared the winner.

The race brought national attention to the AYP Exposition. On a regional level, it brought a new perspective to Snoqualmie Pass. The pass had long been promoted as a railway route, but now it was recognized that it could be a car route as well.

4

One-Lane Road to Superhighway

Unofficial records indicate that 105 cars crossed Snoqualmie Pass in 1909. For several years thereafter, horse-drawn traffic continued to outnumber autos, but the change was coming. A few cars were present in the Snoqualmie Valley from the time of the Alaska-Yukon-Pacific (AYP) Exposition on, and transcontinental auto races continued through the pass for several years. The first car in Fall City — a Stanley Steamer — was evidently driven by William Carmacks, the famous miner who struck it rich in the Klondike. By around 1918, automobiles had killed the livery stable business in the valley, and a number of those proprietors switched to pumping gas.

Toll road days were at an end. Logging and mining traffic had caused portions of the route to be shifted to new localities. On the Kittitas side of the mountains, traffic from North Yakima to Ellensburg still came over the Wenas, but from Ellensburg to Cle Elum the route had changed. The road now crossed the Yakima River about two miles west of the farm town of Thorp — swinging north and away from Taneum Creek — and headed for the Swauk mining camps via Hayward Hill and Horsehead Canyon (now called Horse Canyon). It dropped down to Swauk Creek, then climbed the Ballard Hill, dropped to the floor of the Teanaway Valley, then went west to Cle Elum. Instead of fording the Yakima River at Easton and staying on the south side to Lake Keechelus, the road climbed Easton Hill. For several years, routes on both sides of the Yakima River were used simultaneously. For a while, drivers could choose between the ferry across Lake Keechelus or the primitive one-lane route along the east shore.

Besides logging, which peaked around 1900 at lower elevations, and the mining of gold, silver, copper, and coal, big construction projects also lured thousands of men to the region. First there was the building of the Milwaukee Railroad over the summit of Snoqualmie Pass, then snowsheds were added on the west side of the railroad grade, followed by the railroad tunnel and finally the dams on Lakes Kachess, Keechelus, and Cle Elum. The projects were made possible by the railroads, which brought men and supplies. Though the industrial revolution was beginning to mold the mining and logging industries as well as construction, much of the labor was still by hand. Men fought the harsh overpowering wilderness of forests and mountains first with hand tools, then with horse and steam power, in an environment that repeatedly repulsed travel and settlement.

From 1909 on, settlements on both sides of Snoqualmie Pass yearned for permanent roads that would not be closed by mud and snow in winter. By 1912, there were enough cars in Kittitas County to form an automobile club, which planned to cooperate with similar clubs on Puget Sound to get a good route over the pass. That same year, the state Good Roads Association recommended that three trunk highways be built: a Sunset Highway from Idaho through Spokane, Davenport, Wilbur, Wenatchee, Ellensburg, and Snoqualmie Pass, to link up with the proposed Pacific Highway from Blaine to Vancouver, and the Inland Empire Highway from Spokane through Rosalia, Walla Walla, Pasco, North Yakima, and Ellensburg.

In July, 1912, the *Ellensburg Capital* reported that "Work on Snoqualmie Pass is due to the efforts of King and Kittitas Auto Clubs and County Commissioners of both counties." A large tent resort was proposed for the upper end of Lake Keechelus, which was about half as long as it is now that the water level has been raised. The state began to take an interest in the road, and in September, State Highway Commissioner W. J. Roberts, King County Engineer James Morrison, Kittitas County Engineer Charles Jordan, and others decided that Snoqualmie Pass should have a permanent highway. They recommended a sixty-foot right of way and a twenty-foot roadbed. A conflict developed with those who thought the route should go over Stevens Pass to the north but by December the Snoqualmie boosters had won.

Two men drove motorcycles over Snoqualmie Pass from Seattle to Ellensburg in August, 1913, in the unbelievably short time of twelve hours. Though the road had been improved since 1909, motorists in 1913 still preferred shipping their automobiles over Snoqualmie Summit by train rather than running the risk of breaking down. Motorists paid from $20 to $25 per vehicle to transport their cars over the pass.

About the same time that plans for a permanent road were announced, the state legislature, taking the advice of the Good Roads Association and farmers' organizations, voted $2 million to begin the State Highway Department. Bids were opened in 1914 for twenty-two miles of construction on the Sunset Highway. That summer and the next found a flurry of construction on the highway, and Project Engineer H. A. Murray reported that the crew was rapidly nearing the summit on the west side, clearing trees 5 to 8 feet around and 200 feet high from the 60-foot right of way. On July 1, 1915, Governor Ernest Lister dedicated the route, declaring it Washington's first passable road between the counties east and west of the mountains. A cavalcade of cars

The wagon road along Lake Keechelus in 1911, by now being used by cars.

Asahel Curtis photo, Washington State Historical Society

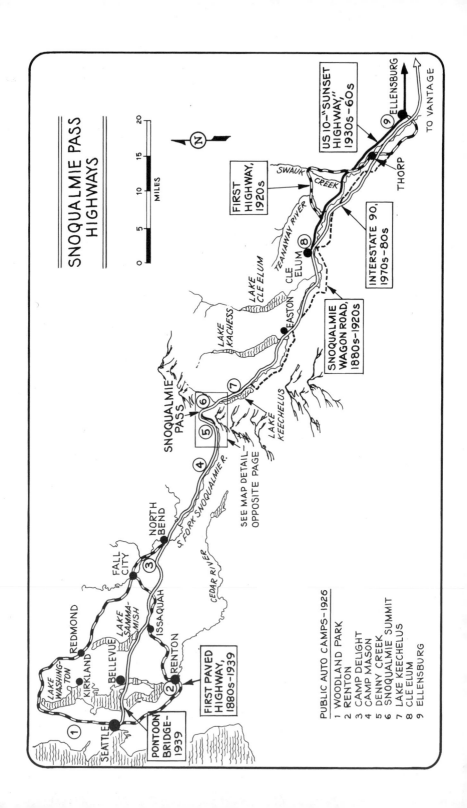

SNOQUALMIE PASS HIGHWAYS

MILES
0 5 10 15 20

N

TO VANTAGE

ELLENSBURG ⑨

US 10—"SUNSET HIGHWAY," 1930s–60s

THORP

SWAUK CREEK

FIRST HIGHWAY, 1920s

TEANAWAY RIVER

INTERSTATE 90, 1970s–80s

CLE ELUM ⑧

LAKE CLE ELUM

LAKE KACHESS

EASTON

SNOQUALMIE WAGON ROAD, 1880s–1920s

⑦

LAKE KEECHELUS

⑥
SNOQUALMIE PASS
⑤

④

SEE MAP DETAIL—OPPOSITE PAGE

S. FORK SNOQUALMIE R.

NORTH BEND ③

CEDAR RIVER

FALL CITY

LAKE SAMMAMISH

REDMOND

KIRKLAND

BELLEVUE

LAKE WASHINGTON

ISSAQUAH

RENTON ②

SEATTLE ①

PONTOON BRIDGE—1939

FIRST PAVED HIGHWAY, 1880s–1939

PUBLIC AUTO CAMPS—1926

1 WOODLAND PARK
2 RENTON
3 CAMP DELIGHT
4 CAMP MASON
5 DENNY CREEK
6 SNOQUALMIE SUMMIT
7 LAKE KEECHELUS
8 CLE ELUM
9 ELLENSBURG

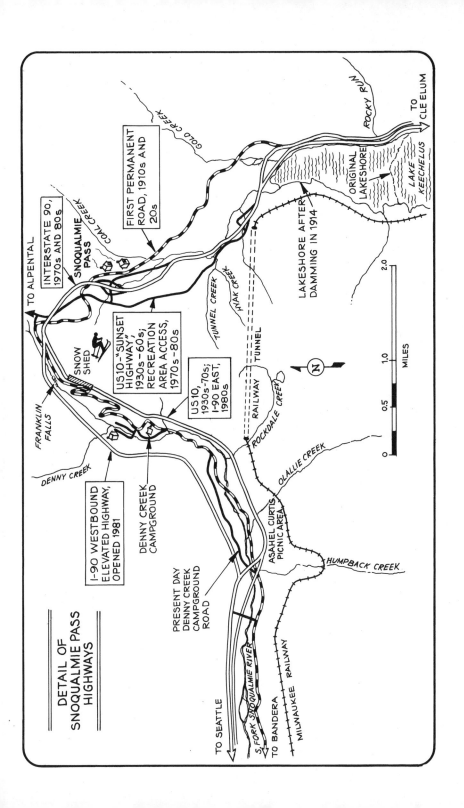

DETAIL OF SNOQUALMIE PASS HIGHWAYS

TO ALPENTAL

INTERSTATE 90, 1970s AND 80s

SNOQUALMIE PASS

FIRST PERMANENT ROAD, 1910s AND 20s

GOLD CREEK

COAL CREEK

ROCKY RUN

TO CLE ELUM

LAKE KEECHELUS

ORIGINAL LAKESHORE

LAKESHORE AFTER DAMMING IN 1914

SNOW SHED

US10-"SUNSET HIGHWAY," 1930s-60s; RECREATION AREA ACCESS, 1970s-80s

US10, 1930s-70s; I-90 EAST, 1980s

TUNNEL CREEK

HYAK CREEK

RAILWAY TUNNEL

FRANKLIN FALLS

DENNY CREEK

I-90 WESTBOUND ELEVATED HIGHWAY, OPENED 1981

DENNY CREEK CAMPGROUND

PRESENT DAY DENNY CREEK CAMPGROUND ROAD

ROCKDALE CREEK

OLALLIE CREEK

ASAHEL CURTIS PICNIC AREA

HUMPBACK CREEK

N

0   0.5   1.0   2.0
MILES

TO SEATTLE

S. FORK SNOQUALMIE RIVER

TO BANDERA

MILWAUKEE RAILWAY

Northwest Collection, Suzzallo Library, University of Washington

Left, *the road west of the pass, along the Snoqualmie River, in 1913.* Above, *the "Sunset Highway" near Snoqualmie Pass, about 1920.*

from Seattle drove to the summit and on to Lake Keechelus in five hours, where they were joined by similar groups from Ellensburg and Yakima.

On hand were Seattle Mayor Hi Gill, Ellensburg Mayor S. H. Kreidel, county commissioners, automobile club members, and state and county engineers. Governor Lister told his audience that the state would continue to lay more gravel and improve the transmountain route for several years, but that there would be no permanent pavement until money was on hand to pay for it. The road would also be maintained as funds came in — that year was the first that motor vehicle fees were set aside as a permanent fund for highway maintenance. It was another seven years before gravel surfacing was finished all the way to Ellensburg.

The 1909 AYP Exposition with its transcontinental automobile race had captivated the imagination of Northwest residents. Big expositions and automobile touring became fashionable simultaneously. World War I had closed Europe to American tourists and the residents of the eastern states were beginning to look westward for travel and touring. Northwest automobile and road boosters were looking ahead to the 1915 San Francisco Exposition. They worked quickly to open and improve both the cross-

Above, *Maloney's Grove, and Peter Maloney, proprietor. This privately run car camp-ground east of North Bend operated from the 1920s to the 1950s. Below, the AAA's Pon-tiac truck used in road service on Snoqualmie Pass, 1930. It led the first convoy of vehicles over the pass when the road opened after the winter of 1930.*

state route through Snoqualmie Pass and the north-south Pacific Highway with access to Mount Rainier, hoping to attract eastern and midwestern auto buffs to detour through the Northwest either en route to or from the Exposition. Although the number of travelers that actually took the detour was only in the low hundreds, the efforts served to improve the road greatly.

Over 1,000 people attended the Washington State Good Roads meeting held in Ellensburg in the fall of 1916. The father of the good roads movement, Samuel Hill of Maryhill, Washington, presented a color slide show, including slides of the lavish, scenic wonders of the Northwest. Slides of Snoqualmie Pass ranked in beauty with those taken in Europe, the Columbia River Gorge, and the Oregon Coast.

In 1926, the Mohawk-Hobbs Rubber Company of Akron, Ohio, published and distributed a travel guide for the highway, *Yellowstone Trail, Seattle-Chicago, Grade and Surface Guide*. According to the guide, the road distance from Seattle to Cle Elum was 101.3 miles. The road was paved from Seattle to Bryn Mawr, near the southern tip of Lake Washington. From Renton to Fall City it was "fine wide cone" and from Fall City to Ellensburg and Yakima, it was gravel and dirt of varying degrees. There were not as yet any motels, although there were a few inns, but many auto campgrounds were springing up. The Mohawk-Hobbs guide listed Woodland Park Camp in Seattle at 50 cents a night; Renton had a car camp; and Camp Delight was near the town of Meadowbrook. Farther into the mountains were Camp Mason, Denny Creek Campground, a camp at Snoqualmie Summit, another on the shores of Lake Keechelus, and tourist auto camps in Cle Elum and Ellensburg.

The Highway Department began making plans for changes to the roadway in 1926. It would be free of blind curves, and there would be pavement, new bridges, and relocations of portions of the road. The Milwaukee Railroad had by this time constructed a tunnel and vacated its old right of way over the summit, and it was soon announced that a new road would follow the old right of way. Summit switchbacks would be eliminated and seven new bridges would be built between North Bend and the summit. The Cle Elum–Ellensburg section would be relocated to follow the course of the Yakima River through Cle Elum Canyon.

Through the 1920s, Snoqualmie Pass was being opened just a little earlier each year as the road crews were supplied with

A sporty roadster along the "Sunset Highway" in the 1920s.

more, bigger, and better equipment. The usual date was in late May, and the final snowdrifts were opened by blasting with dynamite.

Morris Jenkins, who arrived in Easton from Idaho in 1929, was one person who worked on the highway. He got a job working on the highway for the Johnson Brothers contractors. He recalls:

> The first job I had was raking the fat rocks off the highway. The fat rocks were oversized river gravel. That first fall I worked from Cle Elum west to the Cle Elum River, then from Easton about up to Midway Park up over Easton Hill. It was all handwork. We used wheelbarrows, shovels, and rakes. On the project we were building

up the shoulders of the roadbed, and it was all done by wheelbarrow. Guys were filling up wheelbarrows where they had lots of dirt and wheeling it where it was needed. We'd make fills and then smooth it off with rakes. There were at least twenty of us. Every night we'd hide our wheelbarrows out in the woods and then get them the next morning. Each man was responsible for his own tools and had to replace them if lost. A lot of the crew was transients — you'd call them hobos — and we made 50 cents an hour. The most you could work [in one day] was nine to ten hours. Then they'd charge 6 bits to $2 a day for room and board, so it didn't leave you very much. I came in October and worked until it closed down for the winter about the first of December.

Jenkins pointed out that this was finishing work; by then, the Highway Department had started to use bulldozers for the primary construction. He recalls the highway as a narrow, gravel, one-way road that was fine in dry weather, but in wet weather the wagons sank clear to their axles in mud.

After spending the winter trapping, Jenkins returned to work on the Sunset Highway. He said, "I went to work up by Lake Keechelus where they did a lot of blasting. They used to drill holes and keep shooting them out until they got a dent. It was called a coyote hole. Then they would load dynamite by the whole boxes in there and blow a series of those. I used to flag traffic then. When they'd set that off there'd be a tremendous explosion and it would blow the whole mountainside off. It even blew rocks clear across the lake to the Milwaukee (Railroad) side."

He went back to Idaho and was married. The cere-

During snow clearing on the pass, April 1921.

Automobile Club of Washington

Automobile Club of Washington

Sometimes the horseless carriages had to resort to real horses to get through the snow!
June 27, 1916.

mony was performed by a justice of the peace, who asked where
the couple was headed. Upon hearing that they were going back
to Snoqualmie Pass country, he told them that he used to herd
cattle over the trail in the 1870s and that it was rough on the
cattle. He said the cattle almost went berserk in the timber because of the narrow trail, biting flies and mosquitoes, and devil's
club and that every time they made the trip, they lost a few animals. He figured that even after all those years, Jenkins might
yet find an old cow's skull high up in the rocks somewhere. A
few years later, while running section lines high on Keechelus
Ridge, Jenkins did find an old steer's skull green with algae and
age.

Between 1934 and 1936, about forty-seven new bridges were
built on the Snoqualmie Highway. The famous pontoon bridge to
Mercer Island across Lake Washington was completed in 1939,
shortening the route considerably. The bridge charged tolls from
1940 to the late 1950s, when it was finally paid for.

Above, *steam shovels were used to clear snow in the spring of 1921.* Below, *this was labeled "Opening of Snoqualmie Pass," springtime, around 1920.*

Above, *Day's Service Station at Snoqualmie Pass, January 3, 1927.* Below, *the Snoqualmie Pass road west of the summit, near the Milwaukee Railroad trestle, about 1917.*

Al Schober collection, Cle Elum

Above, *summit of Snoqualmie Pass in winter. The first year the pass was open all winter was 1931-32. Below, tractor and grader at work on Sunset Highway southeast of North Bend, 1919.*

King County Department of Public Works

The road along Lake Keechelus in the 1930s. Note paving.

Hay truck crosses through the pass in the mid 1930s, on a two-lane concrete roadway. Highway crew is at work on right.

In 1934, Governor Clarence Martin dedicated the first paved road, a seventeen-mile concrete ribbon, through Snoqualmie Pass. Concrete snowsheds were added in 1950, and in 1952 work on a concrete four-lane route was begun on the west side of the pass. The highway was an important military supply line during World War II, but travel was limited to thirty-five miles per hour. After the war, as cars were being built to travel faster, the road was altered to accommodate first a fifty mile-per-hour speed limit, then seventy in 1963. The limit dropped back to fifty in 1973, but in the intervening ten years, the drive from Seattle to Ellensburg took about one and one-half hours. The speed limit rose again in 1974, but only to fifty-five miles per hour.

Plans for even more lanes of traffic and straightening of the kinks in the route were begun in the late 1960s, but they were held up for a number of years due to environmental concerns, which resulted in changes in construction techniques. The new five-mile section from Denny Creek Campground to the summit was laid in 1970 and contains some of the most unusual construction techniques in North America. To protect the roadbed, there are rock gabion structures — essentially large wire baskets filled with boulders — above and below the highway. There is a 3,620-foot-long Franklin Falls–Denny Creek viaduct, constructed at a cost of $13 million. To preserve the forest and mountain landscape as much as possible, builders have used a movable scaffold system which does not require ground support, to build the bridge — that alone cost almost $1 million. One construction hazard has never changed, however: all projects cease during the winter months.

No doubt the changes to the roadway will continue. There are always new plans for development of the pass area, including more skiing areas, a 600-room hotel with revolving restaurant on top, and trams to the summits of Silver Peak, Lundin Mountain, and other highpoints. The pass is adjacent to the Alpine Lakes Wilderness Area to the north and therefore is a crossroads of heavy motorized traffic on I-90 and foot and horse traffic flowing north and south over the Pacific Crest Trail.

Landowners at Snoqualmie Pass include the Forest Service, the Milwaukee Railroad, Burlington Northern Railroad, Boise-Cascade Corporation, Ski Acres, The Mountaineers, and others. There is no question that there will be more changes at Snoqualmie Pass. The only question is: What kind?

5

The Changing Towns

The richest resources along the Snoqualmie Pass route have been mining, farming, timber, and recreation. Early arrivals, however, had great visions for an industrial empire built on the mineral wealth to come from the summit of Snoqualmie Pass itself. Some of the dreams and schemes have been realized, some half realized, and some never got off the ground. Other dreams — particularly the skiing empire — were beyond imagining in the early days. Towns were established, grew, and sometimes dwindled as a reflection of economic developments. The earliest settlements began about the same time in the two river drainages whose headwaters are at Snoqualmie Pass — the South Fork Snoqualmie to the west and the Yakima to the east.

Probably the first permanent white settler in the Snoqualmie Valley was Jeremiah (Jerry) Borst, who arrived in 1858 or 1859 and homesteaded 160 acres on Ranger's Prairie, using the buildings of old Fort Alden at first and later those of Fort Smalley.

Borst kept adding to his land until he owned several hundred acres; he was the first to start hop farming in the area. In addition to farming, he operated a small trading post. Supplies came from Seattle, which meant a three- to four-day trip by canoe and trail up the Snoqualmie and Snohomish rivers in the early days.

When livestock drives through the pass began in 1869, Borst's place became a popular stopover on the way to Seattle. The cattle could rest and gain back the weight they had lost in the several days of trailing over the narrow, rocky defile through the mountains. Other homesteaders in the valley also leased pasture, and several families provided board and room for the weary drovers.

Apparently, Borst learned of iron deposits at Snoqualmie Summit from his Indian wife. In 1869, a mining expedition was organized on his farm, and with an Indian guide, a group of Seattle men — including Arthur Denny — prospected on the Middle Fork Snoqualmie River. The men kept their findings quiet until a few years later when the Denny Iron Mining Company was established. The discovery of what they thought would be paying lodes of iron ore at Snoqualmie Pass, and the knowledge of existing coal mines in the mountains and near the salt water, later formed the basis for the dream of a large iron ore smelting center. The dream launched a railroad and several Snoqualmie Valley towns, but the industry never developed. The mining prospects did, however, contribute to the pressure for a decent road over the pass.

In 1882, Borst sold much of his acreage to the Hop Grower's Association, which expanded the ranch until it was the largest hop-growing site in the world. Figures on the ranch's size vary, but it was certainly over 1,000 acres, with several hundred in hops. Very soon, there appeared a cookhouse, rooming house, trading post and post office, barns, and kilns. The ranch prospered and attracted a large labor force of Indians from around the territory and from as far as British Columbia during harvest season. Harvest lasted three or four weeks, and the kilns ran around the clock. Most of the hops were sold to Germany and England.

In the mid-1880s, there was a hotel built on the farm, which became well known as the Meadowbrook Hotel. It was carpeted and furnished with oak and walnut pieces shipped from the East. Its guest register, which is now on display at the North Bend museum, contains such names as A. A. Denny, David Denny and wife, Dexter Horton, Governor Elisha P. Ferry, Mrs. David Maynard, Bailey Gatzert, Henry Yesler, and Peter Kirk. The hotel was used as a resort for about twenty years, serving as a base for hunting, fishing, and driving through the fields to watch the hop pickers.

The hop industry ended disastrously in 1890 as a result of seriously fluctuating world market prices and the arrival of the hop louse, which devastated the crop. Today, few realize that hops were once a popular crop west of the mountains. Near Fall City, however, there still stands a protected old hop shed as proof.

Jeremiah W. Borst, who homesteaded in 1858 (where North Bend is today), and established a hop ranch which became the largest in the world by the 1880s.

The first permanent white settlers in the Kittitas Valley were Frederick Ludi and John Goller, who arrived from Montana in 1867. There had earlier been two missions, one near Union Gap and one south of Ellensburg, but both had been abandoned by 1855 because of Indian wars.

The third settler was Tillman Houser, who had farmed about six years near Renton. In 1868, he built a cabin north of what is now Ellensburg and returned to Puget Sound via Snoqualmie Pass for his wife and family, improving the wagon road as he went. With him on the first crossing were William Kiester and Christian Clymer, who had herded 500 head of sheep east through Snoqualmie Pass. Clymer chose to continue his residence on the west side of the mountains, leaving his sheep in the care of the other men.

That same year, Fielding Mortimer Thorp and Charles Splawn brought their families north from the area east of Yakima, and homesteaded on the Taneum Creek, twelve miles west of what is now Ellensburg. They opened a small trading post, which, like Borst's place west of the mountains, was the last stopping point on the way to the pass. Until Thorp and Splawn arrived, communications across the mountains had been extremely unreliable, but the two men initiated the first mail route over the pass. They hired an Indian named Washington to make weekly mail trips to Seattle, for which they paid him $10 per round trip. They discontinued the service two years later when they could not persuade residents on the west side that they should pay half the

Mill at Thorp is the town's oldest surviving building.

cost. Splawn also began the first school in Kittitas County. Classes were held at the homestead; the first students were all Indian children. Today's I-90 passes over the ancient Indian trail between Cle Elum and Ellensburg and goes right by the old Thorp-Splawn homestead on Taneum Creek, where travelers can still see the land and small family cemetery of these early settlers.

The Kittitas Valley, with its thousands of acres of bunch-grass grazing, was becoming known as cow heaven. In 1870, Andrew Jackson Splawn, Charles Splawn's brother, and Ben Burch began a trading post that became known as Robbers Roost (now Ellensburg), and Andrew soon bought out Burch. The post was built on a big campground where the cowboys stayed during the summer, gathering the cattle for trailing over Snoqualmie Pass, and it was supplied by wagon, team, and packtrain from The Dalles, Oregon.

The disastrous rain and floods of the winter of 1869–70 had washed. out many sections of the Snoqualmie Wagon Road, closing it to wheeled traffic. In 1871, John Shoudy of Seattle rode through the pass on horseback as a representative of Seattle interests who wanted the road rebuilt. With the intention of buying out Jack Splawn, Shoudy took two wagons from the Kittitas Valley to Seattle in October with the help of William Fawcett. They rebuilt the wagon road as they went west. They stocked up with supplies and returned before the first winter storms. Then Shoudy bought the trading post. The following year the pass was again closed to wheeled traffic, so the post was supplied by thirteen packtrains that went to Seattle and back. Travel was still so difficult that when Shoudy sent for his family, they came by way of Portland, The Dalles, and Yakima.

Trade went well, and in 1875 Shoudy laid out a town, selling home lots at $2 apiece and business lots at $10 apiece. He named the town in honor of his wife, Ellen, and became the town's first postmaster as well as a member of the territorial legislature in 1883. It was through his influence that Kittitas County was formed; his picture is still displayed over the counter in the Ellensburg post office.

The discovery of gold on Swauk Creek in 1873 and along Peshastin Creek in 1874 greatly increased the amount of traffic moving east through Snoqualmie Pass. The little village of Meaghersville (now Liberty) sprang up on the Swauk, and Blewett was founded on the Peshastin side of the mountains. Both Blewett Pass and the town were named for Edward Blewett, a mining engineer from Seattle.

In the early 1880s, steam navigation developed on the Snohomish-Snoqualmie river system from Puget Sound north of present-day Everett, and steamboats made it as far up river as Snoqualmie Falls on occasion. The town that is now Fall City and other landings were established along the route.

By 1884, it was known that the Northern Pacific was finally going to finish its Cascade section, which would cross the Columbia River from the east, proceed up the Yakima Valley nearly to the foot of Lake Keechelus, then turn west over Stampede Pass to Tacoma. The first logging camps — in effect, temporary towns — in the upper Yakima-Kittitas watershed were built at this time. The camps were established in the area from the Teanaway to above the Kachess River (now Lake Easton), and hundreds of men were employed to cut timber to supply the lumber for the building of the Northern Pacific bridge over the Columbia and ties for the railroad line. Logs were floated down the Yakima River to Ainsworth (now Pasco). When the railroad began building its switchback over Stampede Pass, and later its tunnel under the pass, more logging was done to supply timbers for the bridges and tunnel.

The founders of present-day Cle Elum were Walter Reed and Thomas L. Gamble. When coal was discovered in the vicinity in 1884, they established homesteads and later platted the townsite, giving it an Indian name meaning "swift water." Prospectors were pouring into the area. The Northern Pacific sent men and equipment to explore, and they found a rich deposit of coal just north of Cle Elum, where Roslyn is located now. Many of the miners, loggers, and others attracted to the booming region arrived via the Snoqualmie Wagon Road, on foot, on horseback, and in wagons.

Roslyn was platted in 1887 by Logan M. Bullitt, vice president of the Northern Pacific Railroad. He named the town after either Roslyn, New York, or Roslyn, Delaware — whichever of the two circulating stories you wish to believe. For a time, Roslyn rivaled Ellensburg in importance.

There was a serious mine strike in 1888 in Roslyn, which crippled operations and led to violence in the community. There were beatings and a general fear for personal safety. The company imported two trainloads of black workers from Illinois to break the strike, and for a while the black population in the community outnumbered the white. Over the years, the black population has died out or moved away. In 1975, Willie Craven,

Ellensburg cheese factory, late 1890s.

Ellensburg Library collection

a gravedigger and a member of the only remaining black family, was elected mayor of Roslyn, thus becoming Washington's first black mayor.

Considering its size, Roslyn has one of the strongest ethnic mixes in the state. The Northern Pacific brought in immigrants by the trainload — Croatians, Scots, Italians, Yugoslavs, and many others. A retired Roslyn schoolteacher recalls that she once had members of at least twenty-two separate nationalities in her classroom.

A visit to the town's historic cemetery will reveal Roslyn's rich past — actually, it is over twenty small cemeteries adjoining each other. There are ornate tombstones, neatly fenced enclosures, outlines of whitewashed rocks, and other symbols of the varied makeup of the community. As in many small towns, the descendants care for the plots. Many of these descendants live in the Puget Sound region and make a pilgrimage the week before Memorial Day to spruce up and decorate the graves. It is a nostalgic, festive occasion, and sometimes families can be heard talking in their native tongue, reciting family history to their children.

Roslyn reached its peak population of about 4,000 during the 1920s, in the years of the largest coal output. Coal was king in

Clarence Palmer's livery stable, Ellensburg, early 1900s.

Ellensburg Library collection

both Roslyn and Cle Elum for many years. In the early years before the immigrants could speak much English, they worked together in their own ethnic groups in the mines. Frank Musso, who worked many years in the mines, is today the person who cares for the Roslyn Museum, which is small but rich in heritage. He can tell many exciting, firsthand stories about life and times in the early days of the town.

There is a striking contrast between Cle Elum — now the larger of the two towns — and Roslyn. Cle Elum looks like the usual western town with a frontier background, while Roslyn has an old world rustic charm. The original Snoqualmie Wagon Road had branches through both towns. There was a ford across the Yakima River at Cle Elum for access and another trail through Roslyn, skirting the foot of Lake Cle Elum and climbing over Easton Ridge.

Coal ceased being mined in the late 1950s for large-scale commercial use, due to a combination of high production costs and changing patterns in fuel use. For a time, because they had such deep roots in the Cle Elum–Roslyn communities, men who had formerly been employed in the mines refused to move their families. They sought jobs in Seattle and commuted daily through Snoqualmie Pass to work. Now, however, new economic patterns have developed, such as the booming ski industry. Most have either found nearer places of employment or have moved away, and a new population is moving in.

One of the boom towns that appeared and disappeared about the time Cle Elum and Roslyn were developing was Teanaway City, about seven miles east of Cle Elum where the Teanaway River joins the Yakima. Though short lived, the town had a colorful history. It was platted by Henry Ortley in 1886, and at one time it had thirty buildings and a store operated by Theron Stafford. For a while it had its own post office and later was a railroad stop. Its founders believed it would soon become large and prosperous, adding to both railroad and wagon road traffic.

In 1884, even before it was a town, one of the local residents, Fred Seaton, decided to put out a newspaper to serve the surrounding farm area. The *Teanaway Bugle* was one of the earliest newspapers in the area, and among its advertisements was the following:

Ellensburg – view of Fourth Street looking west, about 1910.

PARTNERS WANTED! MUST BE FEMALES!! BEAUTY NO OBJECT!!! After roaming around this cold, cheerless, and unsympathetic world for many years, with nothing to love, no one to caress us, we, the undersigned old bachelors, have at last settled down on lovely ranches in the charming valley of the peerless Teanaway. All that is wanting to complete our happiness is partners of the female persuasion. No capital required and but few questions asked. Women of uncertain age and questionable beauty acceptable, provided they can otherwise pass examination. Sound teeth and strong constitutions are the essential requisites. Address either S. L. Bathes, J. B. Moore, C. M. Giles, Colonel Mason, Ephraim Allyn, T. L. Gamble, Gus Pletet, N. Plaisted, H. Boardwell, S. A. Bacon.

At least three of the gentlemen found marital bliss as a result of this advertisement.

When the Northern Pacific chose Cle Elum as its rail headquarters, Teanaway City closed up practically overnight. Today, the Teanaway Junction Cafe is a nearby landmark, and the railroad has a sign for Teanaway, just across the road. Otherwise, there are no surviving buildings.

Another early dream of industrial might gave rise to Kirkland. Clarence Bagley, in the chapter "Kirkland-Redmond" of his *History of King County*, put it well:

Above, *Central Hotel in Cle Elum, popular with rail passengers and auto tourists in the 1920s.* Below, *Cle Elum in the early 1900s—note mud street.*

The account of the rise and collapse of the Kirkland steel bubble reads like fiction. The great industrial city that was projected on the eastern shore of Lake Washington was the talk of the Puget Sound region in the late 80's and early 90's. To utilize the ore (from the Denny Iron Mines at Snoqualmie Pass) which was believed to exist in paying quantities a huge iron and steel works, with smelting plant and shops for the fabrication of rails and other steel products would have to be built somewhere on the Sound. L. S. J. Hunt of Seattle, owner of the *Post-Intelligencer*, about the year 1887, conceived the idea of erecting this plant at Kirkland. He transmitted much of his enthusiasm to Peter Kirk, who for many years had been engaged in the manufacture of steel products at Moss Bay, England. The plan was to mine the ore in the Snoqualmie Lode, owned by A. A. Denny, and ship it to Kirkland for reduction to steel. The proximity of limestone and coal to the Denny mine was expected to provide a cheap product which would make Kirkland the center of a steel industry that would be able to undersell eastern points.

Peter Kirk and another English iron manufacturer, Walter W. Williams, came to Seattle and spent two years studying the project in the mid-1880s. They then leased the Denny Iron Mines for forty-five years. According to Bagley, L. S. J. Hunt bought acreage now included in Kirkland, then organized the Kirkland Land and Improvement Company and the Great Western Iron and Steel Company, which were primarily controlled by the same people. Hunt transferred his property to the Kirkland Land and Improvement Company.

A broader view of Kirk's dream of tapping mineral wealth via the railroad is told in the book, *A Report on Washington Territory*, by Dr. W. H. Ruffner, L.L.D., published by the Seattle, Lake Shore and Eastern Railway in New York in 1889. Dr. Ruffner visited Snoqualmie Pass in 1887, coming into Washington Territory via the Northern Pacific Railroad to Tacoma, then by boat to Seattle, by rail to Newcastle, and by horseback over the wagon road east to Snoqualmie Pass. He was accompanied by F. H. Whitworth, an engineer, and F. M. Guye, a local iron mine owner. He made his visit in October and hurried so he would not be stopped by bad weather. Even so, he covered quite a bit of ground.

He noted the work being done to extend the Seattle, Lake Shore and Eastern Railway beyond the hop ranch to the vicinity of the mines and visited the Guye Iron Mines a mile north of the pass. He noted outcrops of ore and limestone high on a mountain that he called Mount Logan in honor of General T. M. Logan, whom he recognized as being among the first eastern men who put faith in the resources of this remarkable region. The mountain is now called Guye Peak.

Ruffner stayed a night at the engineers' camp, then stopped to see activities at Sallal Prairie. Here he found a large camp of employees of the Moss Bay Iron and Steel Company, of England. They expected to build iron furnaces at this location, but Kirkland was soon decided upon as a more logical site. On his way back to Seattle, Ruffner reported staying at the "Hop Ranch," probably the former Meadowbrook Hotel near the present-day town of Snoqualmie, and the next day he visited the Raging River coal diggings. Then he visited the Gilman Coal Mines, now the town of Issaquah, and spent the night nearby at Tibbetts' Hotel. Before meeting Peter Kirk back in Seattle, Ruffner also found time to visit the completed portion of a locally built railway, as well as the Wilkeson Coal Mines, which were located between present-day Buckley and Orting northwest of Mount Rainier.

He was in Washington Territory, barely touching Oregon, for a little over five weeks. Whitworth accompanied him on all his travels outside Seattle, and he was given a thoroughly guided tour and provided with reams of statistics and maps of the area. Ruffner was greatly impressed with the timber resources he saw, and in his book, he stated:

> The forest of mill timber beginning in sight of Seattle, continues with some intermissions to the top of the Cascade Mountains. It increases in size and quantity to a point far up on the mountain side, and the trees continue of good size all the way to the top.
>
> The sun never touches the earth in these forests. The trees rise to the height of 250 feet or upward, and lock their branches together far overhead, shutting out the sunlight and awing the traveler.

Besides being impressed with the timber, Ruffner felt the route of the railroad through Snoqualmie Pass would tap the coal fields at the Gilman mines, Raging River, Snoqualmie Pass, and Roslyn. It was thought that there was another rich bed of iron ore, north of the Roslyn–Cle Elum coal beds near Lake Cle Elum, and there was talk of mining it as well. Ruffner left the territory uncertain where Kirk planned to build his steel mill, but certain that the development was soon to come.

Instead of building an industrial center at Sallal Prairie or Cle Elum, Kirk chose the town that is now named for him. Seattle stockholders in the industrial plan for Kirkland were Edward Blewett, L. S. J. Hunt, Jacob Furth, C. T. Tyler, Peter Kirk, W. W. Williams, and Bailey Gatzert; and the town was platted in 1888. A boom was on because the Seattle, Lake Shore and Eastern was being built toward Snoqualmie Pass, and manufacturing equipment for the steel mills was sent over from England. A workforce erected several large brick buildings in Kirkland, and all the northwestern region was astir with the project. There were plans for a blast furnace, rolling mills, and a workforce of 1,000 men. There were eastern investors in the project as well.

The great dream was destined for failure, however, for a combination of reasons. The iron ore deposits were not as rich as first believed and could not be mined cheaply. Also, the panic of 1893 struck at a crucial time and the financial backing crumbled away. Kirk had invested heavily and was very disappointed in the outcome. He lived for a time in Kirkland, then moved to an island in the San Juans, where he died in 1915.

The town of Kirkland revived after 1900 and has grown steadily since that time. For many years eastside commuters took the steamboat ferry *Lincoln* between Kirkland and Seattle. It was supposedly the largest fresh-water ferry in the West, with a capacity of fifty cars and thousands of passengers. It ended service in 1940 when the Mercer Island–Lake Washington Floating Bridge was built.

For a time it looked as though Kirkland might outstrip Seattle and Ellensburg in growth, as both of the latter towns had suffered disastrous fires in their business districts in 1889. Today the town is proud of its history and has preserved the Peter Kirk building, which is used for the performing arts. Kirkland still has a Moss Bay, named by Kirk after the site of his industrial plant in northern England, though the present bay is much changed. In 1916, the Lake Washington Ship Canal was built, connecting the lake to Puget Sound. The water level of Lake Washington was lowered nine feet, and Moss Bay was reduced to a mere inlet. In some places in Kirkland, it is still possible to see traces of the old sea wall built along the lake's former shore.

Moss Bay is also the site of a historic boat collection, open to the public in summer. One ship, the three-masted schooner

Wawona, is the last of its kind and is now a national historic site. Hundreds of pleasure boats are also moored there at Marina Park, and there is a shopping district and a park nearby. It is sometimes hard to regret that Peter Kirk's dream of industry failed.

The leaders of Seattle evidently had confidence in themselves during this period. Despite the fact that the city had not yet become a railroad terminus or even received a reliable railroad connection, it was growing. Fishing and timber products had produced successful trade. The thousands of cattle that had been driven through the Cascades over the Snoqualmie Trail during

the 1870s and early 1880s had created a major meat-packing industry, and canned and cured meat was shipped out on steamers up and down the Pacific Coast, even to the Orient. Much of the wagon traffic of new immigrants to the region poured westward through Snoqualmie Pass, once the cattlemen opened the toll road in 1883. Seattle was also the major outfitting point for Klondikers during the Alaska Gold Rush that began in 1898.

The expectation of eastside industrial development was another lure, and the proposed Seattle, Lake Shore and Eastern Railway Company made plans to build a branch of the railroad north to Sumas to link the Canadian Pacific with the branch

North Bend in 1906 – Bendego Street and First Avenue, looking east. Note loaded pack train.

Snoqualmie Valley Historical Society

William H. Taylor, as King County
commissioner in 1888. Taylor
founded town of North Bend.

around the north shore of Lake Washington out to Issaquah in
order to tap a coal mine there.

Daniel H. Gilman was the early hero of this venture. Seattleites
financed his trip to the East Coast to seek out funds, and it was a
success. The company was incorporated on April 15, 1885, with
$50,000 of local money and $450,000 from New York. The new
railroad had reached Woodinville by late fall of 1887, and logging camps, mills, mines, and towns mushroomed in response to
the construction project. The railroad headed onward toward
the Gilman Coal Mines — an area of yet another confusing suc-
cession of community names: Squawk or Squak, Gilman,
Olney, Issaquah.

The little community located near Lake Sammamish, then
known as Squak, was platted in 1888 by Ingebright Wold and
called Englewood. Nearby were the Gilman Coal Mines, and that
site was incorporated as a town in 1892. The post office was
called Olney, however, because there was already a Washington
town named Gilman. By the late 1890s, local sentiment favored
an adaptation of the Indian name, Issaquah. Today, the Gilman
name remains in Gilman Village, a shopping center in Issaquah,
constructed of relocated sawmill-town buildings and housing a
variety of specialty shops and restaurants.

The railroad made it easier to get to Seattle from the Issaquah
area. Before this, there had been a stage line operated by George
Tibbetts from Newcastle to Squak and then North Bend. An
alternate means of travel between the two areas was to pole a
canoe or scow along Lake Sammamish, through Sammamish

Slough to Lake Washington and the wharf at Fleaburg (now Leschi). From there, there was a wagon (later a trolley) that crossed over the hill into Seattle.

As the railroad was built beyond Issaquah, more and more Snoqualmie Valley towns were platted — Fall City by Jerry Borst in 1887 and North Bend (then called Snoqualmie) in 1889. Although the railroad was spawning the development of logging and of towns along the route, the backers were counting most on hauling ore for a source of revenue, which did not develop as planned. By 1890, the railroad reached Sallal Prairie, at the foot of Grouse Ridge, near present-day Ken's Truck Town, but it went no farther.

Remnants of these days remain in Kirkland, Issaquah, Fall City, Roslyn, and other local communities. There are the three-day Labor Day rodeo in Ellensburg; folklife festivals at Marymoor Park in Redmond, north of Lake Sammamish on the Sammamish River; a logging show each June in Fall City; Pioneer Days in Cle Elum over the Fourth of July weekend; and other fairs and festivals. Museums and historic sites on both sides of Snoqualmie Pass are also available for exploration.

The Milwaukee Railroad depot at North Bend about 1912.

Snoqualmie Valley Historical Society

6

The Inns

Snoqualmie Pass travelers were quickly recognized as prospects for a business opportunity. Even before cars began to appear on the scene, roadside inns and resorts sprang up along the route. They were situated every ten miles or so, strung out from North Bend to Ellensburg. Camp Mason and High Valley were on the west, the Summit Inn at the summit proper, and on the east slope, Lake Keechelus, Sunset, and Rustic inns — all in the vicinity of Lake Keechelus. There was also a gas station at the top of Easton Hill, known as Midway, and old-timers remember the Kachess Inn on Lake Kachess.

The inns could not survive once high-powered cars could make it through the mountains without needing to refuel. Today, the locations of most of the inns lie buried under the lanes of the improved highway. The state Department of Transportation has a highway maintenance shop where Camp Mason used to be, near the Tinkham Road exit off I-90. Camp Mason's early history stretches back to the era of horse and wagon travel over the Snoqualmie Wagon Road, to a young Englishman named Charles Beard.

Not long before the turn of the century, Beard set out on horseback from eastern Washington to Seattle by way of Snoqualmie Pass, a journey of several days. When he reached Mountain View (now North Bend), he discovered that Jack Bush and Jack Moore had established a trading post and constructed a toll bridge over the South Fork Snoqualmie River. He found the scene rather inspiring, retraced his path about fifteen miles to a clearing on the banks of the river, and set up a homestead. He split out slabs of cedar to construct a bridge, built a gate, and felled trees to block other possible crossings of the river. He carved the name of his new camp, Bide-a-Wee, on a large cedar and was open for the summer's business. It was mostly covered-wagon immigrants and herds of horses, cattle, and sheep heading west over the pass.

Among his first customers were a preacher and his family. They had expected to rest for a few days, but the loss of a horse stranded them for some time longer. Beard put the family to work building a few log huts. They were floorless and windowless; meals were cooked over a fire built on the ground in the center of the hut. (Most women travelers of the era could bake good bread in a frying pan over an open fire.)

Before the summer was over, the bridge was paying its way, and Beard had several huts plus a barn for storing hay. The hay was harvested mostly by Indians who were on their way to the west side of the mountains for the hop harvest. They cut armloads of loose hay and tied them with a few long stems of grass wrapped around. They looked like the bundles left by the combine binder of today.

By this time, the preacher had bought another horse from a passing trader and was ready to move on. His daughter, however, was ready to marry Beard. No license was required; her father performed the ceremony. Bide-a-Wee prospered.

About the time that Beard was tiring of life in the mountains, M. C. Mason came to North Bend with the Milwaukee Railroad building boom, established himself in business, built a home, and married. Transportation was better and faster over the pass, and Bide-a-Wee was becoming a brief pleasure stop rather than a layover of several days. Telegraph service and a post office came to the area. Beard traded Bide-a-Wee to Mason for two houses and lots in North Bend.

Mason built better cabins as well as an eating place and a grocery for travelers. Automobiles were becoming a little more common, and the State of Washington was surveying through Snoqualmie Pass for a new highway. The rest stop, renamed Camp Mason, once again prospered.

The property changed hands several times in later years before the superhighway construction took over. The state acquired the site and the buildings were removed when the highway was widened to four lanes.

The only remaining landmark of the inn era is the former

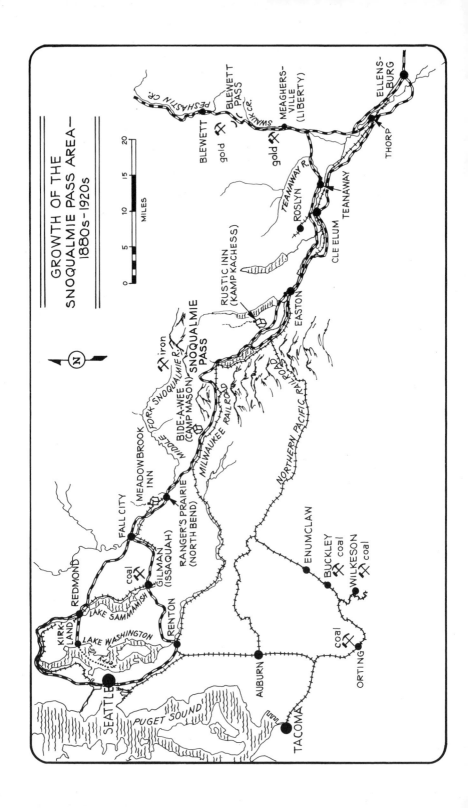

GROWTH OF THE
SNOQUALMIE PASS AREA—
1880s-1920s

N

MILES
0 5 10 15 20

SEATTLE

PUGET SOUND

TACOMA

KIRK-
LAND

REDMOND

LAKE SAMMAMISH

LAKE WASHINGTON

RENTON

AUBURN

ORTING
coal

ENUMCLAW

BUCKLEY
coal

WILKESON
coal

NORTHERN PACIFIC RAILROAD

FALL CITY

MEADOWBROOK
INN

GILMAN
(ISSAQUAH)
coal

RANGER'S PRAIRIE
(NORTH BEND)

MILWAUKEE RAILROAD

MIDDLE FORK SNOQUALMIE R.

BIDE-A-WEE
(CAMP MASON)

iron

SNOQUALMIE
PASS

RUSTIC INN
(KAMP KACHESS)

EASTON

CLE ELUM

TEANAWAY

ROSLYN

TEANAWAY R.

THORP

ELLENS-
BURG

MEAGHERS-
VILLE
(LIBERTY)
gold

SWAUK CR.

BLEWETT
PASS

BLEWETT
gold

PESHASTIN CR.

Rustic Inn, now the site of a private camp, Kamp Kachess. The two-story log structure is located beside I-90 at the Stampede Pass-Lake Kachess interchange. Clovis Chartrand, a man who lived near Ellensburg until his death in 1981, helped build the solid structure and lived in it for some years. Chartrand was born in 1902 and came to the area in 1910 with his widowed mother and his brothers and sisters. His recollections of the early days follow.

Cora Chartrand had been widowed in 1904; she had eleven children and lived in upper Michigan. The woods had been home for her all her life; the men in her family were all trappers or prospectors, and her sons also showed a bent for outdoor living. By 1904, her son Lee was already working for the Forest Service near Snoqualmie Pass (he later became district ranger at Cle Elum), and he urged his mother to bring the family and homestead a meadow along Swamp Creek near Lake Keechelus.

At the time, the only way you could homestead was to claim agricultural land. Someone had started a homestead in the meadow before, but had abandoned it; it had already been surveyed. Though it was only thirty-two acres, it had some good prospects with the highway going through, and Mrs. Chartrand thought it would be worth it. After camping at the site for a time, she filed for a homestead in 1911, and the family began to build, first a log cabin, then three or four log buildings and several frame structures.

They pitched in to make a living on the homestead, selling meals and providing campground accommodations for overnight stays, first for the wagon trade and later for automobile travelers. Clovis later recalled, "We had a huge garden on the meadow, raising our own produce for the cafe my mother operated. The soil was rich along the creek, and we raised all kinds of vegetables. The growing season was real short, but we raised rutabagas and cabbages that were huge — some weighed twenty pounds. We had our own milk cows and horses and raised our own grain and hay for the livestock."

After work began on the dam on Lake Keechelus around 1911, the family peddled milk in the construction camp two or three miles away. During the summer months, Mrs. Chartrand drove a two-wheeled cart and took whole milk in bottles, carried in a box that slid under the seat; it held two dozen quarts. The winters were too long to keep livestock at the homestead, so the family

Rustic Inn, now site of a private camp 10 miles east of Snoqualmie Pass, was built by the Chartrand family about 1930.

pastured the livestock out for the winter or sold them and bought others the next summer.

Mrs. Chartrand spent winters in Cle Elum with her oldest son's family. Until 1915 when he went to high school in Cle Elum and even for some winters after, Clovis stayed up at Lake Keechelus with the project engineer's family. From time to time in the winter, he and the engineer's son went by snowshoes or skis to the Chartrand homestead to shovel snow off the roofs of the buildings. Sometimes the trip took four hours because of the heavy snow. They made their own snowshoes, using horsehide for lacing. Between trips for shoveling snow, they would set snares for rabbits.

Clovis recalled that during the winter of 1915-16 they had a very deep snow. He and two of his brothers were staying up at the lake during the winter that year. They went to the homestead to shovel snow and were afraid the ridgepole on one cabin was carrying too much weight, so they worked all day to shovel the snow off the roof of the twelve-foot-high cabin. First they had to shovel down to the ridgepole to get the snow off; then they had to pack the snow up to surface level. Before they left, they notched a tree at snow level so they could measure the depth the next summer. It was fourteen and one-half feet deep under the tree where they measured, and it must have been sixteen or seventeen feet deep in the open.

Clovis remembered a still-unexplained incident that happened during his childhood, when he and a younger brother were across the wagon road from their property, playing in a little campground with a big stump beside it.

We looked down the road and saw a man on horseback coming up the road just a laying her wide open. He was laying right down over that horse. When he got to within about two hundred yards of us, we seen another man come around the turn. There was a straight stretch in front of us through here about half a mile long. He took two shots at this guy coming down the road so we climbed up on the stump to get a better look at what was going on. We were about ten and twelve years old then. They both went by here just lickety-split and this guy took another shot at him with a pistol. In four or five minutes, here come something else down the road — it was a great big bloodhound. His ears were flopping. He was following the deputy. And we never did find out who they were or what was happening. There was no newspaper or radio then. If we could've seen a newspaper down in the valley, it might have told something, but we didn't. We got our news from one person telling another or going to the post office and receiving a letter.

Clovis also remembered a big dam-construction camp at the lower end of the lake, called Meadow Creek. There was great activity there in the summer, with hundreds of men staying in bunkhouses. At about age thirteen, Clovis worked for a short time in one of the mess halls as a waiter. He recalled perhaps

Sunset Lodge near Keechelus, built between 1910 and 1920.

1,500 men there, in bunkhouses strung through the woods — "we'd call them tarpaper shacks now"—with bathhouses between some of them. In summer, Meadow Creek's population was 1,500 to 1,800 and it had named streets with street lights. It had a post office, school, store, YMCA, and other businesses. In winter, all activity came to a stop because of the snow. All the workers left with the first snowfall and only twenty-five families stayed to maintain the camp and shovel snow. The Chartrand brothers walked there to school in the winter.

There was a railroad station on the Milwaukee, also called Meadow Creek, where supplies for the dam construction came in. The camp had a narrow-gauge railroad that ran across the top of the dam where the men hauled rock and material and dumped on both sides. There were 500 head of horses and mules on hand for moving the dirt.

Someone at Meadow Creek experimented with putting snow-shoes on horses while Clovis was attending the Meadow Creek school, but apparently only three ever got so they could handle themselves well. Blocks of wood about eighteen inches square were used for the shoes, attached with an iron bridle that fit over special horseshoes made longer so they stuck out and could be attached to a clamp.

There was one large horse that wore these snowshoes; he was a pet and would go around to everybody's house, and people would feed him bread and potato peelings and other scraps. One day the kids were in school when they heard a racket outside. The teacher sent Clovis out to see what was happening. The snow was so deep that a trench had been dug alongside the windows to let light in. The boy climbed up a snowbank where he could walk to the top of the school roof, and there was the horse—he had walked to the top, snowshoes and all, and somehow had avoided falling in the ten-foot-deep trenches.

A team of small black horses also handled themselves well on snowshoes, except that they stepped on each other. Except for those three, all the horses were taken out in the winter.

When the Chartrands first lived on the homestead, eight to ten teams would come by in a week, and one car in a month. It seemed to be mostly working people passing by, and they would stay at the little campground across the road.

The Chartrand family would often see cattle and hogs being driven through. It was quite a chore to get some of these outfits

Clovis Chartrand, right, his niece Cora Jean, center, and sister Catherine, about 1920.

Some horses were equipped with these special snowshoes for winter mobility.

Above, *Keechelus Inn in winter, about 1935.* Below, *the Meadowbrook Hotel, located along the river near the town of Snoqualmie. It was operated from about 1886 to 1914, then until 1948 was a rooming house.*

Summit Inn, about 1925.

on the ferry that operated on Lake Keechelus. The ferry was a big scow with a railing on it, and it was about long enough for a wagon and a team. People would unhook the horses and tie them to the railing, then block the wagon so it would not roll off. Ordinarily the ferry would not take loose animals; they had to be driven on the narrow road along the east side of the lake.

The Chartrand family lived in a log cabin at first. Then they had two log cabins with a kind of hallway in between; they used one as storage for fuel in winter. One cabin had a fireplace; the other was more like a bedroom and had a stove in it.

About 1912, Mrs. Chartrand opened the Doughnut Shop between the two cabins, and soon became well known for her specialty — homemade doughnuts and hot coffee. People would drive up from Cle Elum and Seattle and buy four or five dozen, which they could eat there or take out. When she was making doughnuts, you could smell them half a mile away, according to her son. She supposedly used an old Salvation Army recipe, but she never passed it on to anyone. She used about half a dozen big skillets on a wood stove and fried the doughnuts in melted lard, turning them with a fork as they sizzled. She served them plain, not sugared. The coffee came from the three to five percolators that were kept going all the time — percolators were fairly new then, and people raved about the coffee as much as they did about the doughnuts.

As motorized traffic became heavier, the Chartrands opened a gas station and grocery store and cleared space for a campground across the road (where Crystal Springs Forest Service Campground is now). The boys cut fenceposts and sold them to truckers, operated the gas station, and helped in the grocery store and the Doughnut Shop.

The present log structure known as Kamp Kachess was built by Clovis' brother Ed in the 1930s. Clovis helped his brother with the construction over a period of six or seven years. They cut cedar trees in Swamp Creek flat; the foundation logs were three feet through and are as solid today as the day they were put in. The lodge was built as a restaurant, hotel, and home. Beautifully finished inside, it had an upstairs with numerous bedrooms arranged around a balcony. The fireplace was originally eight feet wide and people could sit inside it.

At the same time the lodge was being built, Ed installed a dam on Swamp Creek, creating a small lake in the summer. The original water supply for the lodge came from a spring connected to the building by a two-inch wooden pipe, later replaced by a two-inch iron pipe. Eventually, a well was drilled, which is enclosed in a corner of the lodge.

The Rustic Inn, only ten miles east of Snoqualmie Pass, attracted many travelers. There was a toboggan and ski hill behind the lodge, which Ed and some Seattle friends operated for about three years in the mid-1930s; it attracted people from the coast, Ellensburg, and Cle Elum. The original toboggan hill was carved out of the snow and ice. It was a long, fast ride with the runout on the Swamp Creek flats. A rope tow was used to pull people up both the toboggan hill and the ski slope. There was a platform at the top, and a lever was tripped to get the toboggan ride started. Only one person at a time could handle the slide that first year — there was one place where the toboggan even flew through the air. The hill was later shortened, and two people could ride a toboggan down at one time.

Today's trend of moving from the farm to the city was happening then too. Clovis moved to Ellensburg, got married, and settled in a pioneer home in the Kittitas Valley. The Doughnut Shop is a fading memory, and only a few of the highway's fast-moving travelers know that Kamp Kachess was born as Rustic Inn and that it has been watching the changes in Snoqualmie Pass since the days of horse-drawn travel.

7

The Milwaukee Railroad

The building of railroads through the Cascades was a monumental task, and the Milwaukee, St. Paul, and Pacific Railroad across Snoqualmie Pass was no exception. Men battled both the weather and the mountains. The right of way had to be cleared of timber and stumps; swamps, streams, lakes, and chasms had to be bridged; track had to be laid. In the high country, heavy snows forced work to cease for all but the three summer months.

Even though Snoqualmie Pass was the lowest of the railroad routes, the Milwaukee was the last of the three northern transcontinental railroads to build a track over the crest of the Cascades to Puget Sound. The Northern Pacific went across Stampede Pass into Tacoma, and the Great Northern crossed Stevens Pass into Everett. For years there had been a dream of a railroad directly into Seattle, and this dream was fulfilled in the spring of 1909. By summer, the postal telegraph was following the rail line across the summit, thus revolutionizing communications with the outside world.

On the west side of the pass, the Milwaukee began its climb from the Puget Sound lowlands not far from Cedar Falls and gradually ascended, its roadbed built to cling to the mountainsides on the south side of the South Fork Snoqualmie River. When the line reached a point above present-day Asahel Curtis Campground, it crossed Humpback Creek and ascended to the pass on a grade 50 to 100 feet above today's location of I-90. It descended to Hyak, staying above where the ski area access road is now, then went on the same line it now follows, around the south side of Lake Keechelus to Ellensburg. The stations and flag stops east from Seattle were: Argo, Van Asselt, Black River,

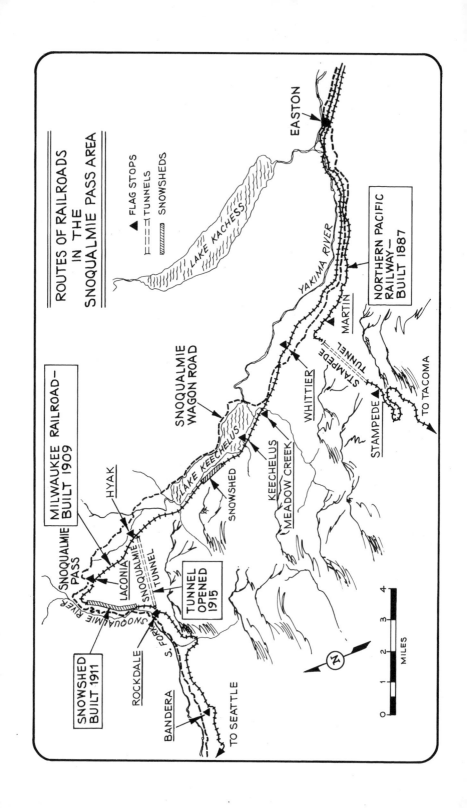

ROUTES OF RAILROADS
IN THE
SNOQUALMIE PASS AREA

▲ FLAG STOPS
══╡ TUNNELS
▨▨▨ SNOWSHEDS

EASTON

LAKE KACHESS

YAKIMA RIVER

NORTHERN PACIFIC
RAILWAY—
BUILT 1887

MARTIN

STAMPEDE
TUNNEL

WHITTIER

STAMPEDE

TO TACOMA

SNOQUALMIE WAGON ROAD

MILWAUKEE RAILROAD—
BUILT 1909

HYAK

LAKE KEECHELUS

SNOWSHED

KEECHELUS

MEADOW CREEK

SNOQUALMIE
PASS

LACONIA

SNOQUALMIE
TUNNEL

TUNNEL OPENED
1915

SNOWSHED
BUILT 1911

SNOQUALMIE RIVER

ROCKDALE

S. FORK

BANDERA

TO SEATTLE

N

0   1   2   3   4
MILES

Renton, Elliott, Cedar Mountain, Maple Valley, Landsburg, Barneston, Cedar Falls, Ragnar, Garcia, Bandera, Rockdale (just west of the summit), Laconia on Snoqualmie Summit, Hyak, Keechelus, Meadow Creek, Whittier, Easton, Lavender, Cle Elum, Horlock, Thorp, and Ellensburg. The line of the old railroad is still to be seen about thirty feet above the freeway, just west of the summit, as it traverses the slope above the snowshed.

The direct route to Seattle increased the flow of immigrants to the Northwest. It also meant that produce could flow both ways over the mountains in greater abundance and with much more ease. Generally, agricultural products flowed west to the Seattle markets from the hinterland of eastern Washington; supplies for home, ranch, and mines were shipped east out of Seattle.

With the completion of the Milwaukee Railroad over the summit in 1909, a new era came to Snoqualmie Pass. Six years later it was improved even more when a tunnel was completed from Hyak to Rockdale, eliminating the steep grade and shortening the route by four miles. Locomotive engines of the period had to take on water every few miles, and passenger trains would stop anywhere. Recreational outings to Snoqualmie Pass originated in Seattle, the various Snoqualmie Valley towns, Cle Elum, Ellensburg, and even Yakima. Thousands of people began enjoying the mountain grandeur in the summer by taking the train and picnicking on Lake Keechelus. Hundreds of berry pickers rode the train in late summer to find huckleberries. The rail route opened a bonanza of outdoor recreation and enjoyment. Each season, when lower fares were instituted for settlers going west, one popular recreation was going to the town train station to watch the immigrants passing through. Today, a group of train buffs keeps steam locomotive history alive in the town of Snoqualmie. The old train depot has been refurbished, and during Christmas and the summer season, a steam-powered train runs a scenic tour near Snoqualmie Falls.

Construction of the railroad also quickened the interest in an improved road over the summit, especially now that the horseless carriage had appeared on the scene. From the early days when the pace car for the New York–Seattle race was ferried through the mountains on a Milwaukee flat car, the railroad's presence has complemented and enchanced the role of automobile travel over the mountains.

Before 1888, miners and anyone else who had a reason to live

Laconia stop on the Milwaukee Railroad, 1909-16, was the summit of Snoqualmie Pass.

in the mountains faced a four- to eight-day trip to get to Snoqualmie Pass from the pioneer communities on either side of the mountains. After the Northern Pacific put its line across Stampede Pass from Tacoma to Ellensburg, the prospectors, hunters, and surveyors could get off at Whittier and hike around Lake Keechelus to Snoqualmie Pass. Or they could ride the Seattle, Lakeshore, and Eastern Railway from Seattle to Sallal Prairie on the west side of the mountains and hike up the wagon road. A trip across the mountains took three to four days by horse and two — under good conditions — by car.

With the arrival of the Milwaukee, travel across Snoqualmie Pass became easier. It took from 6:00 p.m. to 11:00 p.m. to get from Seattle to Ellensburg, and the traveler could choose standard or first class. There were sleeping coaches, dining cars, observation platforms, and drawing rooms aboard the passenger trains. Despite the time still required to get from one side of the mountains to the other, it was faster and far better than the

hazards of horse or car. On straight stretches a train averaged sixty miles per hour, a car twenty. In the more sizable towns, horse-drawn drays met people at the train depot and took them to the local hotel.

Railroad travel also offered year-round service through the mountains, overcoming heavy snows, storms, and conditions that rendered the wagon/car road impassable. Except under the worst conditions, rotary snowplows kept the tracks open, but nothing similar was available for auto traffic.

The winter of 1909–10 was rather bad — that was the winter of the Wellington Disaster at Stevens Pass, where ninety-six people on two trapped trains died in avalanches. On Snoqualmie Pass, the gauge on the Milwaukee line showed 100 inches of snow total. Six feet fell in one storm, the temperature dropped to ten degrees, and there were strong east winds through the pass in a storm that extended from ocean to ocean. Snow fell at the rate of one foot an hour. In the mountains, snow depth exceeded twelve feet in places; it was four and one-half feet at Cle Elum and nine inches in Seattle. It was the worst storm on record. There was no Milwaukee service for ten days — even the rotary snowplows were snowed in.

In 1911, the Milwaukee Railroad added snowsheds to their line over Snoqualmie Summit, between Rockdale and Laconia. Said to be the largest snowsheds ever made on an American railroad, they extended more than a mile and were constructed by traveling cranes that ran on tracks at the top of the sheds. Tent camps were set up at Laconia and Rockdale for the hundreds of laborers.

Ruby Grandstaff of Ellensburg, who served as Easton's postmistress for twenty years, remembers Cascade winters: "One winter we had very deep snow and it was hard getting around, shoveling out paths that were tunnels. We thought, well, next winter will be milder; it couldn't get worse. But we were wrong. Our memories are so short — we think heavy-snow winters are unusual, but they're not. You can have two heavy-snow winters in a row in the Cascades."

Fortunately, the new railroad over Snoqualmie Pass did not have to face that problem immediately. After the difficult winter of 1909–10 there were two milder winters before another that was even more difficult. The road over the mountains was often buried under gigantic snowdrifts and slides that reached forty feet in depth. In April, 1913, an article by William Ennis entitled "Keeping the Road Clear," published in the railroad's company magazine, explained the system of dealing with winter snows. It is easy to say that the snow was more than forty feet deep, and equally easy to shrug off the figure without giving it much thought. But Ennis's story makes you feel the chill:

> Our line crosses at what is known as Snoqualmie Pass, where during seven months of the year we have snowfall, and five out of those seven months it is very heavy, amounting in 1910 to forty six feet on the level, while the present year up to March 1st, we have had forty two feet. We have a record up here, also, of a fall of forty one inches in twenty four hours, of 251 inches in one month, and a continuous storm of twenty six days in January, 1913.
>
> To handle this and keep trains moving requires four rotary plows, operated in pairs, one on each end of a Mallet engine. Laconia is the station on the summit, and from here to Cedar Falls

at the foot of the west slope is twenty four miles, all mountain-grade; from Laconia to Cle Elum on the east side is thirty one miles, and in these two districts we operate the four plows. The snow fall on the west side is much heavier than on the east. In addition, we have an L-1 engine equipped with a flange device on the pilot, to flange the track from Laconia to Cedar Falls. We also have another crew with a K-1 engine for handling laborers. Our winter gang numbers one hundred, who do nothing but shovel snow and work with a machine known as a widener, this being a flat car equipped with two heavy iron wings so set that they will widen the cuts, to give a better clearance. This machine is run in connection with a rotary plow, cutting the snow from each side of the track and leaving it in the center for the plow to throw out to clear.

During storms it is necessary for the plows to precede every train, as in addition to the falling snow, there are constant slides from off the steep mountain slopes.

There is seldom much wind in the mountains during these storms, so that the snow lodges on trees and rocks sometimes staying there for weeks, then when it gets warm or a rain comes, it falls and starts sliding. The snowfall during January of the present winter was so heavy that the weight of the snow alone caused it to slide. When it began to rain, the enormous weight broke the wires down and put the electric signals out of commission, cutting us completely off for four days. It is hard to repair wires in the mountains during heavy snow, as the linemen have to use snow shoes, and in many places must tie ropes around their bodies and be let down over the mountain side by their comrades in order to reach the wires.

To man a double rotary snow plow, ready for service, requires two engineers and one fireman to each plow — one engineer is stationed in the pilot house of the plow, keeps a lookout ahead, handles the levers which work the flangers and transfers signals to the engineer who works the pusher engine. The second engineer runs the engine which drives the rotary wheel. The engineers and firemen of each locomotive and the train crews make up the outfit, which is always ready for service.

At points where slides may be expected, we have watchmen day and night and these men have telephone connections with the foreman at Laconia, being required to report to him every two hours as to weather conditions in his territory. The foreman (or the snow king as he is nick-named) has absolute control of all train movements in the snow district. This was some job during the latter part of December and all through January of this winter, when we had a fall of 17 feet in 26 days, with high winds and lots of

Above *and* below,
*Milwaukee rotary snowplow
working near Laconia, 1916.*

The "working end" of a double rotary snowplow.

rain thrown in. Our worst experiences this last winter occurred during that period. The rotaries had to bore through slides from twenty to forty feet deep, and were several times buried by slides coming down while they were at work in a drift. They then had to be dug out, and a number of times the relief crew had to walk four and five miles over slides and in blinding snow to relieve their comrades, who had worked the limit of endurance trying to keep the road open. The roadmaster, traveling engineer and myself have headed relief parties of this kind, with 75 and 100 laborers, where we had to break a road with each step sinking into soft snow to your waists. We could not use snow shoes on account of frequent slides.

When plows work under these conditions they are veritable furnaces and I know of no hotter place on earth. In order to keep dry, we have to wear a full rubber suit and when you think of that and with winter clothing on, in a cab with windows and curtains drawn, snow banks thirty to forty feet high on each side and two hundred pounds pressure on the boiler, you can gain some idea of what the boys have to go through in order to keep the "yellow cars" moving.

Ennis then describes one of the worst experiences of the railroad in the snowbound Cascades:

It had been snowing for upwards of ten days almost continuously and I had been in hourly communication with the watchmen on the west side. The weather had every indication of turning into a bad night, so I notified the dispatcher to tie up all the freight trains and keep the line open for No. 18, coming from Seattle.

The double plow was ordered to go to Cedar Falls and return ahead of No. 18. East side plows were in readiness to go to Cle Elum, on arrival of the west plows at Laconia. On my way to supper I met two or three of the older men who had spent previous winters in the Cascades and all agreed that it looked like a bad night, but thought we would not have any serious trouble because the snow was light and dry. Promptly at 7 p.m. the boys were ready and started west. Not over 10 minutes before they left, I was talking to Watchman Sloggy who is stationed near our worst slide territory. He had just been over the bad district and reported everything O.K. I told him the Bull Moose (meaning the double plow), had just gone west and to look out for them. Hardly had the plows gotten out of hearing when the phone in my car rang as if the party on the other end was trying to tear it off the wall. It was Sloggy, who said that from the noise it made, he thought the whole mountain must be down in Snoqualmie Canyon, and it was still roaring. While he was talking, a small slide came down and struck his shack, nearly upsetting it. It was too late to get hold of the plows and there was nothing to do but wait, as I could not send after them to warn them of conditions. It was nearly 11 p.m. before I got any word of them, although Sloggy said he could see them hard at it, and it looked as if they were nearly through the worst of it. About 11:15 Sloggy said they had stopped and he thought they were covered by a slide, as he could see some lanterns approaching. Shortly, Traveling Engineer Buchanan called me and said they were caught, and it was still sliding. They had a good crew of shovelers, but we called out the reserves and started for the trouble. The snow had slid in behind the plows for over two miles, making progress of the relief plows very slow. Fortunately before the night was over, it turned cold, which stopped further sliding, and we were able to get to them, after which we soon had them out and started for Cedar Falls. I then ordered the relief plow to Cle Elum, as reports were coming in of slides on the east side, and I did not hear from them again until I had reached Cedar Falls....

It was still snowing and the following afternoon started heavier than ever. Westbound passenger trains were away late, and so about 7 p.m. I ordered the plows to Cedar Falls after No. 18, although I did not think it could slide again after all the snow which had come down the night before. After receiving advice from all the watchmen, who reported conditions favorable, the boys left. In about thirty minutes one of the watchmen near Rockdale reported slides at a point where we had never before experienced any trouble, and very soon Sloggy reported that it had again started sliding on his beat. I ordered No. 18 held at Cedar Falls, and soon the

Train-load logging on the west slopes of the Cascades in Snoqualmie Valley.

conductor of the crew called from Sloggy's shack that conditions
were worse than the previous night — the plows were covered and
would have to be dug out. No relief crew could be sent on account
of two plows being broken down. We started down to them over
the snow, but could not make any effort to get them out until daylight. This was our worst experience, as the storm was blinding
and we sank waist deep with every step. We had to make nearly
three miles thus on foot, but after six hours of hard work at digging, we got them out and started for Cedar Falls. Everyone was
pretty well tired out, walking and shoveling, as every man —
engineers, firemen, conductors and brakemen — had taken their
turn at the shovels, so I asked if they wished to tie up for rest, but
not one of them would think of such a thing as long as the line
was blocked. We coaled and watered and got a good meal for the
men and started back. Superintendent Foster joined us, which
gave the boys additional spirit, and it was needed, as we found
conditions just as bad as they had been on the downward trip. We
got along fairly well as we had increased our push power with
another Mallet engine. At Rockdale we found it was getting colder,
with a high wind. With a fresh supply of coal and two firemen
working on the plow, we started for Laconia. We found every cut
full — wherever it could slide it had not failed to do so, and the
snow was drifting ahead of the high wind and freezing hard. This
made hard work for the plow and we were over six hours going
four miles. Engineers, firemen and some of the rest of us were
nearly suffocated with the heat. The pilot house of old rotary No.
20 was the hottest place I have ever seen. The old men who had

Eastbound electric-powered freight train in Snoqualmie Pass about 1939-40.

fought snow in the Dakotas and Minnesota, back in the '80's say they never put in as bad a night and day as we had passed through. When the linemen got out and got one wire working, we got word that other transcontinental lines would not be open for several days. When the men learned this, you could hear many such remarks as this: "They can't stick us, even if we are new in the west" and "Guess we will run as many trains as the rest of the roads if the machinery holds out."

The Milwaukee Railroad had done some surveying for a tunnel as early as 1908, and preliminary work had begun in 1911, but it was that winter of 1912–13 that clinched it: construction of a tunnel under Snoqualmie Pass would begin in earnest as soon as weather would permit. Boring was completed August 5, 1914, and the first train went through in an appropriate season — January 24, 1915.

Tunnel workers, known as "tunnel stiffs," were a tough breed of men who followed tunnel construction work all over the world. Many were Caucasian, but there were also Orientals and Indians in the crews.

Daily progress on the tunnel was posted each night where the men could see their results, and there was strong competition between those working on the west and east ends of the tunnel to see who could get the most drilling done in a day. The sounds of construction included the drills, the men's hoarse shouts from inside the tunnel bores, the dump cars, and dynamite blasts. Again, the article by Ennis presents the picture of what the work was like:

> An advance heading 8 feet high by 13 feet wide was driven at sub-grade and to one side of the tunnel section, the work being carried on continuously by three shifts of men who worked six hours and laid off twelve. Each shift consisted of four drill runners, four helpers, ten muckers who worked six hours, and a shift boss, nipper and heading skinner who worked twelve hours. These men were paid on an hourly rate, in addition to which was a bonus of an hour a foot for all progress over ten feet a day, the work being measured every ten days. When the rock was good, bonuses were often made and the average progress for 6971 feet of bottom heading was 9.5 lineal feet per day with a maximum of 25 lineal feet in a single day.
>
> The work in the heading was divided into several operations, all being preparations for blasting, the average time between shots being sixteen hours, but under ordinary conditions, a shot was fired about every twelve hours. Two and one half to three [hours] were spent in breaking down the roof in the part just blasted and in pulling back the broken rock from the face of the heading to allow the drilling to proceed. Seven hours for setting up the drill cross bar and drilling the 14 to 30 nine-foot holes required to break the rock. One hour clearing the drills, loading and shooting. One hour waiting for the heading to clear of gases. While there were many exceptions to the above, it was the general program followed day after day until the east and west headings met.

The tunnel stiffs removed 180,000 cubic yards of rock during the fifteen-month construction project and used 340 tons of dynamite, exploding 100 rounds at a time. The tunnel was lined with 75,000 cubic yards of concrete, which required many yards of gravel and 500,000 sacks of cement, in addition to all the lumber, hardware, and other materials for forms.

The two-mile tunnel under Snoqualmie Pass was a major construction accomplishment. It is not surprising that many of the tunnel stiffs — wearing their accustomed outfit of rubber boots, a slicker, and a souwester — were on hand to welcome the train full of dignitaries that January day when the tunnel opened. The train's arrival signaled the opening of Snoqualmie Pass to reliable year-round travel.

8

Personalities of the Pass

Many volumes could be written about all the people whose lives have been interwoven with Snoqualmie Pass. There are the trappers and traders, the miners and cattle herders, the keepers of stables that turned into gas stations, the settlers headed west who passed by once and never returned. This chapter offers only a tiny sampling to add a little flavor to the contrast of the remnants of the wagon road and today's rushing lanes of cars and trucks.

There is, for example, Catherine T. Maynard, who used to ride over the pass on horseback. She had come across the Plains in a train of covered wagons and had lost her first husband to a cholera epidemic along the way. Dr. David Maynard was part of the same train, and upon their arrival in Seattle, the two were married after he divorced his first wife, who had remained in the East. Doc Maynard was Seattle's first doctor, lawyer, justice of the peace, notary public, storekeeper, commercial fisherman, and Indian agent. From him, Mrs. Maynard learned the skills of nursing and in many ways knew as much as any pioneer doctor when it came to nursing the sick back to good health. She operated a "lying-in apartment" in connection with her husband's hospital. After his death in 1873, she briefly operated a reading room for the public. She was relieved of her volunteer effort by the establishment of the YMCA.

Apparently, Mrs. Maynard had property of her own in Medical Lake in eastern Washington and Ellensburg. Her trips across the pass to these locations began around 1875. Historian Thomas Prosch, in his book *David S. Maynard and Catherine T. Maynard*, commented that she made "her trips over the mountains on horseback as though she were a young woman of 20 to 40 years instead of the mature woman of 60 to 80." She signed in frequently as a guest at the Meadowbrook Hotel and also stayed with families east of the mountains. "Auntie Maynard" was a valuable person to the early pioneers when there were no doctors in eastern Washington, and Kittitas old-timers remember her most for being the attending midwife at many births. She is also remembered for donating land to Masonic Lodge #39 of Ellensburg, although the temple built there was destroyed in the 1889 fire.

Edna Fleming, an old-timer now retired to Yakima, wrote a book titled *Ah Kittitas!*, in which she recalled with fondness Auntie Maynard's visits. On one occasion, Mrs. Fleming's uncles — at that time two teenage boys who were neighbors of Auntie Maynard — decided they wanted to ride horseback through the mountains to visit their married sister — Mrs. Fleming's mother — in Ellensburg. Their family wanted them to ride in the company of Auntie Maynard because she was so well acquainted with the trail, but being young and impatient, they decided to slip off on their own a day early. They were having a rough trip about the second or third night on the trail. The weather had turned bad, it was cold and pouring rain, and their horses were slipping and sliding in the mud. Like many a weary traveler, when it came time to bed down, they simply rolled up in their blankets beside the trail for the night.

Mrs. Fleming recalls, "They were sleeping when they were suddenly awakened by something shaking their feet and a voice coming at them. Out of the darkness came Auntie Maynard's reproving voice: 'Foolish boys starting on a hard trip all alone. Going to bed with your wet feet, you'll catch your death of cold.' And she got them dried out and no doubt dosed them with some of her medicinal supply. They were lonely boys and were overjoyed to have her finish the trip with them and only too happy to travel back to Seattle with her when she was ready for the return trip."

It is said that Mrs. Maynard introduced the dandelion to the Northwest. Some people are probably not a bit grateful for that, but Auntie Maynard undoubtedly knew it to be a plant with curative and nutritional value. Many people, during hard times or in seeking out natural foods, have found that the dandelion is a tasty salad ingredient. The sight of that bright yellow flower

Catherine T. Maynard, 1865.

University of Washington Libraries

blooming each spring all along the route of Snoqualmie Pass is a delightful reminder of a bright spirit who added great depth and quality of life to the Northwest.

Another interesting person who traveled back and forth through Snoqualmie Pass was Francis Marion Streamer, who was a former Indian agent on the east side of the Cascades. He lived in the Kittitas Valley in the 1870s and 1880s and was a school-teacher, justice of the peace, promoter of the Snoqualmie Pass Wagon Road, friend of the Indians, and free-lance writer, whose articles appeared in many Puget Sound and eastern editions of newspapers. Before coming west, Streamer had for several years been city editor of the Chicago *Times*.

Though Lake Chelan, north of Wenatchee, has long been touted as the Switzerland of America, Streamer coined the phrase in the 1870s to describe the lakes and mountains in the vicinity of Snoqualmie Pass. (This area was set aside in 1976 as the Alpine Lakes Wilderness Area.) He also called the Kittitas Valley a Garden of Eden and from his earliest writings was promoting the trading of farm products of the Kittitas Valley for goods from the Seattle market.

On one occasion, Streamer walked south from Skagit County near the Canadian border through Snohomish and King counties and east over Snoqualmie Pass to the Kittitas Valley and on to seven other valleys or farming areas throughout central Washington. It was a 1,000-mile hike, and from that experience he wrote glowing, firsthand accounts of the benefits of trade through Snoqualmie Pass. He was a veritable early-day, one-man chamber of commerce when it came to extolling the virtues and positive values of a well-developed wagon road through the mountains. These excerpts, from a lengthy letter published in the *Seattle Post-Intelligencer* on July 4, 1877, are typical.

> The object of this last trip was to become more thoroughly conversant with Washington people, and their wants. I knew the country was wonderful in all that constitutes agricultural, mineral, forest and fishery wealths: and I also knew, that proper exertions for the speedy development of all these resources were not being put forth and that several local and selfish interests were overawing the general welfare. I gave considerable attention to Walla Walla, and sought to divert attention to a through daily mail route from Seattle to Walla Walla, overland, by stage, across the Snoqualmie Pass, and urged a petition to Congress for an appropriation to a Territorial or Government wagon road therefor. That met with favor, and struck a new key to unlock the present bar to the inter-commerce between Seattle and Walla Walla cities.
>
> You must commence your part of the road work this summer, and your merchants should subscribe liberally thereto. Open the road to the summit, by the way of the old trail, known to Jerry Borst, and the old settlers; and thus avoid the various river crossings; have a firmer and easier grade; shorten the distance fifteen miles, and construct a good wagon road at a cost not exceeding forty thousand dollars; which you can pay in groceries and merchandise to your hundreds of now unemployed laborers and working people, who would be glad of such an opportunity to work.
>
> When that road is opened, you will then tap the entire country over which I have traversed, and draw to your city the immense trade and traffic of all Washington east of you, and a great part of north Idaho, that looks to the Sound as its natural outlet and commercial center. As it is, Portland gets all this trade by way of the Columbia river, and even the people of this valley [Kittitas] are opening a good level road to Priest Rapids, only thirty miles distant, and with good landing on the Columbia river for steamer to Portland. Seattle cannot afford to lose this trade, which it will if it does not move to save in time. A word to the wise ought to be sufficient.

The letter was signed "Shy-Low," Streamer's pen name. Another letter the same month added: "It will be your railroad

line seven years hence, but you must tap the valley by a wagon
road now or lose all the trade of the Kittitas, Wenass, Yakima,
Natchez, Simcoe and the Walla Walla district — which are great
grain valleys."

Various others of Streamer's letters push for development of
the Kittitas Valley as cattle-ranching country, and for improvement of the wagon road as the most logical route for getting the
cattle to market. During this time, individual work parties com-
posed of cattle interests took the initiative to clear the road
whenever weather conditions permitted. An 1880 description of
using the road, taken from Streamer's personal diaries, sounds
appalling today:

> For a distance of thirty miles from eight to twenty feet of snow
> had to be shoveled out of the old trail; fallen fir trees of pon-
> derosa size and massive hulk had to be cut out of the way; new
> trails made around lake Kitchelos through fourteen feet of snow;
> mountain marshes to be cordurized; old creek washes to be filled
> in; swollen streams to be swam; bottomless quagmires to be
> floored over, and almost every species of the rude freaks of
> naughty nature in her attempts to kick old winter out of the lap of
> gushing spring, to be met here and there, and stoutly contended
> against, but not so rejoicingly overcome. To do all this work,
> clearing trails, quite a large number of Indians have been
> employed for the last three weeks, and they have rendered faith-
> ful service amid the most forbidding circumstances of wind and
> weather, rain, and roar of torrent, day and night, and no faltering
> or looking back.
>
> The inaugurating, outfitting, and expense of this opening out a
> highway to Seattle, is to be credited to George F. Smith, who be-
> longs to that tribe of workmen who know no such word as fail;
> who claims to be more of an "old rustler" than an "old settler" and
> who believes more to putting up Indians to work, then in putting
> them down....

Peter Wold's story is, in many ways, that of a typical settler. He
was born in Norway, where he learned to be a shoemaker, and
moved to Chicago in 1862 to take advantage of this young country's opportunities. Things were going well, so he persuaded his
two brothers, Ingebright and Lars, to join him in the shoemak-
ing business in San Francisco. From there, they moved on to
Seattle and in 1866 opened the first shoe store in the town. Both
Peter and Ingebright bought lots in Seattle. Then, in 1868, the

Mr. and Mrs. Ingebright A. Wold

brothers bought 160 acres in the Squak Valley, cleared the timber, and planted hops. Eventually they employed over 100 Indians and some white families. The general store on the farm was supplied by scow from Seattle.

Peter sold his interest in 1871 and moved to the Kittitas Valley, where he homesteaded. He helped build two blockhouses near Ellensburg for protection of the settlers during a period of Indian scares. In 1881 he and another rancher began the first irrigation in the valley by digging a fifteen-mile ditch from their farms to First Creek on the west end of the Wenatchee Mountains. In 1891, he married Sarah Digen Belgum, a native Norwegian, and they lived out their lives in the Kittitas Valley. The farming community he established became known as Woldale. The drive west from Ellensburg on Old Highway 10 goes by the old Woldale School and gymnasium, now remodeled as private homes but listed in the State Register of Historic Places.

The Wold hop ranch became famous in 1885 as one of the first sites of violence against Chinese laborers by both white men and Indians who did not want the competition for jobs. There was similar trouble on the east side of Snoqualmie Pass at the Swauk Mining Camp, where some 500 Chinese were driven from the mines where they had been digging and panning for gold; it was an ugly period in our history. The farm survived the agitation, and in 1887 Ingebright sold out to his brother Lars and moved on to Lake Sammamish, where he platted eighty acres of his land in the town that later became Issaquah.

One of the people who simply did what they had to do was Clara Wasson, the first woman to drive a car across Snoqualmie Pass. In 1914, the route over the summit was a boulder-strewn set of ruts winding through a wilderness of sagebrush, virgin forest, streams, and swamps. Mrs. Wasson was a widow raising three children in Ellensburg, and the occasion for the trip was a Fourth of July rendezvous near the summit with relatives who would drive up from Seattle.

According to the plan, Mrs. Wasson's sister and brother-in-law and their two children, as well as the sisters' mother would drive all the way from Ballard, northwest of Seattle, and meet the family of four from Ellensburg. All would camp overnight at Lake Keechelus Inn Resort at the west end of Lake Keechelus, have a picnic the next day, and return home the day after that.

Though she did not realize it then, Mrs. Wasson had a good background for being the first of her sex to take a car through the rugged mountains. A native of the Kittitas Valley, she was born in a log cabin on a homestead near Taneum Creek in 1878. Her parents had come to Washington Territory from Missouri via wagon train, railroad, boat, and horseback.

Her father, William Killmore, and two other men had hired an Indian guide to take them through the mountains to the Kittitas Valley. They liked what they found, staked homestead claims, and headed back to Seattle for their wives and children. Indian ponies were found for the women and children to ride, and while they were on one of the innumerable crossings of the Snoqualmie River, one of the ponies stumbled and pitched both mother and newborn son into the icy stream. Killmore rescued them, but the incident may have been what led him to feel that horses were dangerous transportation.

Mrs. Wasson's father, and later her husband, refused to use horses for anything but farming. She grew from childhood to young womanhood walking everywhere she went. She did not ride horseback or in horse-drawn conveyances.

Before she died in 1981 at the age of 102, she sat one day in

Clara Wasson, 1916.

her apartment near the University of Washington in Seattle and mused over a century of life. Mrs. Wasson commented, "When I think of the distances we walked, it amazes me. So often I've said to my daughter, 'Look at all the cars that are on this campus, going by here with one person in nine out of ten cars. They don't walk half as far as we did in those early days.'"

After she was widowed, Mrs. Wasson decided it was time to buy a car. She was the first woman in Ellensburg to both drive and own her own car. She said, "In those days, you didn't need a driver's license. I bought my car from Mr. Kelleher, who was the Ford dealer in town. He showed me how to drive it in one lesson on a short loop drive south of town. My only other driving experience before tackling Snoqualmie Pass was a car trip over a wagon road. I doubt that I'd driven twenty-five miles before the trip to Snoqualmie Pass."

The children were a great help on the drive to the picnic. There was her thirteen-year-old daughter, Jo, and two sons, Harold and Glenn, who were eleven and eight, respectively. They were hopping up and down in their seats, telling their mother what to do and what not to do as she drove along. The children's uncle in Ellensburg also had a car. They had frequently gone for rides with him and had seen how it was done.

In those days, the road went west from Ellensburg, north of

the Yakima River out of town through the desert and up over a
summit at the headwaters of Dry Creek and back down through
Horse Canyon to Lauderdale. It then climbed over another high
point, entering timbered country, crossed the Teanaway River
and went on into Cle Elum. After that it was just a dug-out track
winding through the timber. There was not a bit of gravel
anywhere — just a rough track.

After a long, rugged, all-day journey, Mrs. Wasson and her
children reached Lake Keechelus Inn Resort, located about
where the U.S. Forest Service Rocky Run Campground is now,
near the western end of the lake. The Ballard relatives arrived,
and they all rented one of the resort tents to camp in. Mrs. Wasson's daughter Jo recalls, "We slept on fir boughs and cooked our
own food with supplies we'd brought along. We children enjoyed
putting out crumbs for the Canadian jays that stayed around
camp. It was a wonderful time. There was a problem the next
morning. We'd planned to spend the day and head home the day
after. But Uncle Herb discovered his Buick had a broken axle
and he wouldn't be able to drive it back to Ballard. Our two
families talked it over and it was decided that Grandmother
Killmore and I would take the smaller children across Lake
Keechelus in a rowboat and then catch a Milwaukee passenger
train to Seattle."

Someone rowed the children and their grandmother across the
lake, and they climbed up a trail from the lakeshore to the Lake
Keechelus station, where a train was flagged down. They rode to
King Street Station in Seattle, then caught a trolley to their home
in Ballard. It was a very long day, but they reached home before
the car travelers did.

The rest of the group rode in the Wassons' car. "I really did
not want to drive across Snoqualmie Pass." Mrs. Wasson later explained, "I tried to get my brother-in-law to do it. But he said,
'No, a Buick is a lot different from a Ford. I wouldn't know a
thing about a Ford. You drive and I'll sit in front.'"

She started out and somehow managed to stay on the road.
She remembers meeting some sort of motorcycle at the pass. He
tooted at her to get out of the road for him, but the road was
only a couple of ruts, so she did not move aside. When she got
right up to him, he jumped out of the way. Later, a dog ran in
front of her, and she hit it but did not dare stop. She said, "I just

Old-fashioned power takes this Buick roadster and buggy train over Snoqualmie Pass, 1916.

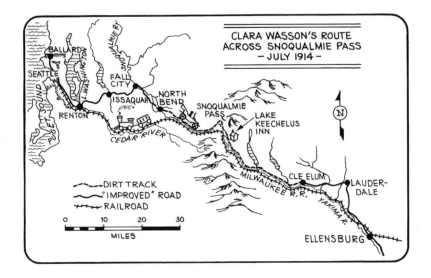

CLARA WASSON'S ROUTE
ACROSS SNOQUALMIE PASS
– JULY 1914 –

kept going until we got there. I remember driving across the old plank bridge, laid on a trestle, to Ballard. My relatives lived just a short ways from that bridge, and we made it safely."

The reunited families rested for a few days. One of them returned to the stranded Buick with a spare axle, repaired it, and drove it home. While staying at her sister's house, Mrs. Wasson read in a Seattle newspaper about a woman who claimed to be the first woman to "navigate" over Snoqualmie Pass. The date was four days after her own drive.

The Wasson family still had to return to Ellensburg. By good fortune, they discovered that some neighbors were also in Seattle, so they could motor back with them in a two-car caravan. It had rained all the time they were in Seattle and the road was bad going back. Just west of Snoqualmie Summit, on the steepest part, there were men stationed with horse teams to pull out the cars that got stuck. The neighbor advised Mrs. Wasson not to stop at that part, no matter what. The ruts were as deep as the Ford's high wheels could handle, and Mrs. Wasson gave it the gas and just hung onto the steering wheel as they spun through the mud. They made it without having to be pulled out.

The two families spent a night at Lake Keechelus Inn and reached Ellensburg after a two-day trip. Mrs. Wasson recalled that her hands were blistered from the trip and said, "I was so exhausted. I don't think I tackled Seattle again very soon after that, but it was a glorious ride."

When Morris Jenkins arrived in the small mountain town of Easton in 1929, he was looking for summer work to put himself through another year of teacher's college in Lewiston, Idaho. Low farm wages back home had driven him to buy a well-used 1913 Model T Ford and set out to seek his fortune. He stopped in Easton simply because he liked the looks of the country.

He looked first for work in a logging camp, but he did not have and could not afford the required calk boots. Eventually, he landed a job on the new highway being constructed over Snoqualmie Pass to replace the existing gravel road, known both as the Yellowstone Trail and the Sunset Highway. He joined a crew of "muckers" who did mostly finishing work with shovels and wheelbarrows. The pay was 50 cents an hour, and with room and board costing at least $1.75 a day, it was hard to save much. Jenkins and his roommate, Warren Haase, were nearly the same age. They became close friends and teamed up together. When the highway construction closed down for the winter, they realized that finding another job at that time of year would be difficult, so they decided to go trapping for furs. They spent about a week looking for a place to trap, before meeting Lawrence Davis, caretaker of the Mountain Goat Lodge on Lake Keechelus at the mouth of Roaring Creek. He told them he had once built a small cabin at Mirror Lake, 1,000 feet higher than Lake Keechelus and about eight miles southwest of Snoqualmie Pass, and that they were welcome to use it.

The two would-be trappers pooled their money for trapping supplies, snowshoes, bedding, a tin stove, cooking utensils, and groceries. They used Davis's rowboat to ferry supplies across Lake Keechelus from Sunset Lodge on the east side of the lake to Mountain Goat Lodge on the west side. Then they started shuttling by backpack up six miles of trail to Mirror Lake. Before the backpacking was finished, Haase was called home because of sickness in the family. Jenkins continued the task alone.

When Jenkins stopped to rest on the trail back to the lodge one day he noticed that the sky was a dark gray and that the black-tailed deer were hurrying toward the passes where they could drop into the lower Cedar River watershed for the winter. He gave the signs little thought, but the next morning there was more than three feet of snow already on the ground, with more falling. He still had one more load to carry, and although he had never been on snowshoes before, it was evident that the time had come.

The young man was not a complete stranger to the mountains. As a youngster in the Salmon River Mountains of Idaho, he had roamed over many miles of the country north of the Seven Devils Mountains with his younger brother. They had eaten many of the wild bulbs, roots, and plants and had had a mutual agreement with animals: "If they wouldn't eat us, we wouldn't eat them." But they had rarely contended with snow more than knee-deep. This winter of 1929–30 in the Cascade Mountains was to be a totally different challenge.

Davis had told Jenkins that the toe of a large leather shoe would make a good binding for a snowshoe, so he had carried in a pair for that purpose. He cut a section out of each shoe, fastened them on the snowshoes, laced the bindings over the toes of his boot, buckled the straps around his heels, and set out for Mountain Goat Lodge.

The trip was an ordeal. He sank deep into the loose snow, and it required great exertion to make each step with a load of snow on top of the snowshoes. After floundering for half the distance, he took his snowshoes off and wallowed through waist-deep snow the rest of the way, arriving at the lodge exhausted. When he arrived, Davis told him that it was always difficult to walk on snowshoes right after a heavy snowfall, but that he had made it doubly so by fastening his bindings on all four corners. They cut the rear fastenings loose, which permitted the heel to drop so the toe could rise above the snow. Jenkins felt both stupid and embarrassed, but he was learning.

That night Jenkins stayed at the Davis place and rested. The next day he rowed directly across Lake Keechelus to Sunset Lodge to pick up his supplies. His partner had just returned, so they rigged up more snowshoes, rowed back across the lake, and snowshoed back up to Mirror Lake, taking turns breaking trail. Although the traveling was mostly uphill, it was far easier than the trip out.

Soon their cabin was completely snowed under. They had plenty of stovepipe, and as the snow got progressively deeper they would add another section to the flue. Some mornings they had to shovel snow into the cabin before they could get a hole up through the snow to shovel it out.

Morris Jenkins in his days as a trapper, 1929.

They solved that problem by covering the top of their burrow with poles and fir boughs and then digging a tunnel in the snow from the cabin door to the edge of the rock shelf on which the cabin was built. Underneath the snow, the cabin became quite cozy. The heat from the cabin melted the adjacent snow, so they could walk completely around the outside of the cabin yet not see daylight because of the snow blanket above. The snow did not even touch the roof; it was like a cabin within a cabin. The only openings to the outside world were the snow tunnel and a hole around the stovepipe. This situation was beneficial, as the temperature dropped to –32 degrees Fahrenheit at Lake Keechelus in early January. It must have been much colder at the cabin. The trees began popping and banging from the cracking caused by the expansion of frozen wood.

On Christmas day each trapper awoke to find that the sock he had hung up for Santa Claus had indeed been filled: Haase had a tin can in his sock and Jenkins had some stovewood in his. They had the best dinner their larder could provide. The next day they headed out to Sunset Lodge for some needed groceries. When they reached the Davis place, they discovered it was

Christmas day — they had celebrated it on December 24. They had Christmas dinner with Davis and his wife, Annabelle. "In all my life," Jenkins recalls, "I've never enjoyed a better meal."

The spring that furnished water for their cabin was located at the foot of a talus slide at the base of Tinkham Peak. They kept the spring open by tunneling down through the snow, but eventually it froze and they had to hike down to Mirror Lake for water. This required more snow shoveling to reach the water in the lake. By the time they had climbed back up the hill to the cabin there would be a crust of ice on the water in their pails.

To make matters worse, mice were coming into the cabin faster than their one mousetrap could handle the traffic. Jenkins remembers being awakened occasionally during the night when a mouse ran across his face.

As they became more expert on snowshoes, the two trappers began expanding their trapline, but by the middle of January, they had caught only two marten and two ermine plus numerous mice and flying squirrels; although their trapline now extended over many miles. It was evident the trapline would hardly support one trapper, let alone two. Haase had a prospect of a job at Rock Island Dam, which was then being built on the Columbia River downstream from Wenatchee, so they bade each other goodbye.

Life became more challenging for Jenkins each day. One day his snowshoe bindings iced up and put pressure on his feet. Although his feet had a strange tingling sensation, he did not realize his toes and heel pads were frozen until he returned to the cabin and took off his boots. Fortunately, he knew to thaw his feet in tepid water. For a time he found traveling difficult, his toes broke into running sores and had to be bandaged. They were very painful, especially when they were warm. The toes finally healed, but the swelling around his heel tendons did not go down for more than six months. Thus he learned that feet should have ample room for circulation in cold weather, but he commented, "The situation might have been worse if I had known about hypothermia. In those days trappers got chilly, or they got cold, or they got damned cold, but they seemed to be immune to the dread disease of hypothermia."

Probably the hardest thing was the solitude. One evening as he neared the lower end of Cottonwood Lake on the way home from his trapline, he heard what sounded like chopping some distance up the mountainside. He figured his partner had returned and was making some more marten sets — the greenhorn would no longer be lonely. He turned off the trail and started climbing the mountainside; there was no answer to his shouts. He had gone some distance when he realized that the sounds came from a large hemlock that was splitting open as the frost penetrated farther into the trunk. Depressed, Jenkins returned to the trail and continued on to the cabin, arriving after dark.

The snow depth was about twelve feet at Mirror Lake and even deeper at the cabin site on a bench above the lake. Even the peak on the roof was under so much snow that the surface above the cabin gave no indication it was there. Only the top of the stovepipe stuck out a bit. One day Jenkins returned to his cabin to find two sets of ski tracks that came down off the ridge above and went right over his cabin, on down the slope, and across Mirror Lake. "There was a set of tracks on either side of the stovepipe," Jenkins remembers, "and I know they never even saw it." He was even lonelier after finding he had just missed two potential visitors.

Crossing Lake Keechelus to get groceries at Sunset Lodge provided some interesting experiences for the young trapper. He used the rowboat until the lake froze solid and then hiked across on the ice from early January until the middle of April. During the three weeks of below-zero temperatures when the lake was freezing over, the cracking and groaning of the ice could be heard for several miles. Davis had chopped a hole one day and measured twenty-two inches of clear ice. One morning, after a spell of chinook weather, Jenkins arrived at the lake to find the ice covered with eight to ten inches of water. There was a riffle over the surface and it looked as if the lake were completely thawed. Knowing the water would not be over his boot tops, he simply waded across. A party of schoolteachers from the Bellingham Normal School, who were spending the weekend at Mountain Goat Lodge, were skiing on the lakeshore. They stared in awe and disbelief as he started across what appeared to be an open lake. Just then a Milwaukee passenger train went by, and the windows flew up as the passengers stared.

The chinook spell had caused cracks to open in the ice, which let water through to the surface. After several days the ice floated to the top again, but it had potholes in it. Now, when Jenkins crossed after dark, he took a kerosene lantern because

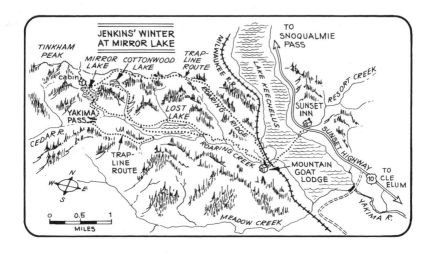

stepping in a pothole could have caused a broken leg.

By mid-April, an open lane extended almost across the lake from Roaring Creek to Sunset Lodge, with an ice island in the middle. Jenkins would pull Davis's rowboat to the edge of open water, row across, pull it up on the ice island, and yell across. The proprietor of Sunset Lodge, Emil Campbell, would row out to the island and take him back for groceries and a visit; afterwards, the whole process would be reversed. One day while Jenkins was rowing across, a strong west wind blew up and began to close the crack. He got out on a shelf of ice and pulled the rowboat out of the water to safety. As the crack came together it began to crush and crumble, shoving ice up in a massive volume. Soon there was a ridge of ice thrust up high all the way across the lake — a regular windrow. Soon, however, it started drifting apart again.

The young trapper learned all kinds of lessons from the environment that snowy, cold winter of 1929–30. As he puts it, "There are many old-timers still living who can remember when Mother Nature ruled supreme over much of the mountain landscape. This was before there were numerous roads and trails, helicopters, snowmobiles, and mountain rescue teams with lightweight equipment. It was a time when those living in the wilderness had a lot in common with the wild creatures. If they were to survive, all had to abide by nature's rules. Most of the wild creatures acquired the necessary skills through instinct, but man had to learn from scratch, sometimes the hard way. However, if he was an alert pupil, he found nature a constant and patient teacher."

Nature was indeed rather gentle in teaching Jenkins about avalanches and cornices. One day as he snowshoed around the base of a small rock pinnacle, there was a boom and the snow broke loose from the face of the rock. He found himself in a seething mass. He tried to run around the slope to get out of the slide, but his snowshoes started to get buried. He rolled to free the snowshoes, then with a fast treading motion started going with the slide while angling toward the edge. Suddenly he saw a tree and caught it as high as he could reach, pulling his feet up until the snow had roared on down the mountainside. He was fortunate; he had been caught near the top of the slide. There were no ledges below, and the tree that stopped him was able to withstand the pressure of the snow. When he looked back up, he was surprised to see he had slid about a quarter of a mile.

Nature had taught him another lesson: Never to get caught in, or even near, a snow-slide area at a time when the snow can be expected to slide. All trappers of that period knew these occurrences as slow slides — "avalanches" only happened in the mountains of Europe. "Had I known I was caught in a genuine avalanche," Jenkins says, "I would likely have died from sheer fright."

A couple of weeks later, while following his tracks from a previous trip along some sheer cliffs above the Cold Creek drainage, he came to a spot where about fifty feet of tracks were missing. They had disappeared over the cliffs when a snow cornice broke off. This time nature's mesage was: When traveling a ridgetop in winter, always walk where the trees grow up through the snow, or if in doubt, keep well to the windward side.

Jenkins also learned some lasting lessons about the problems of extra-deep snow. At the beginning of winter, he left coyote traps set at Cottonwood Lake, but did not pick up the traps when the snow started. It was spring and the snow was about twelve feet deep, before he decided to retrieve the traps. When he finally shoveled his way down to them, he could not get out of the hole. He had to shovel snow back in the hole so he could climb out.

When the snow was deepest that winter, he set out a marten line on Roaring Ridge. He looked for two trees standing fairly close together, wedged two sticks in, trimmed the bark a little,

Morris Jenkins packed supplies and fought fires with the Forest Service for over 14 years.

bent boughs back, and made a lean-to house with boughs over the top so it could not snow in. He put bait in the back end and the trap in the entrance. The snow was about twenty feet deep when he set out the line, and it was summer before he decided to remove the traps. He found them about thirty feet up in the trees.

At the end of the winter Jenkins had a moderate bundle of furs, including marten, ermine, mink, and fox. When they were sold, he had enough to pay his grocery bill at Sunset Lodge and still have a little nest egg. However, his winter resulted in a greater bonus than money. Grover Burch, the district ranger for the Forest Service at Easton, had heard of his experiences from Davis and asked him to stop by.

The ranger said, "Morris, I need a good man for the Big Creek horse patrol. I want a young fellow who can take care of himself in the back country and who won't have to come to town every Saturday night to chase the girls." The Forest Service would furnish tools, telephone, and tent, but he would have to furnish everything else himself — including the horse. His duties would be to detect and suppress fires, to check on sheep grazing, and to enforce Forest Service regulations. He would pack supplies to the Goat Peak Lookout and to any trail crew in the area. From his camp on a high point about halfway from Easton to Green Pass, he could serve as lookout during lightning storms. Since the job would not start until June 15, he got in six weeks' work on the highway, which enabled him to buy a horse, saddle, and other supplies. The summer proved to be the beginning of a long and interesting career in the forestry profession, including fourteen seasons with the Forest Service and thirty years in forest and land management work with the Northern Pacific Railway Company Land Department (now Burlington Northern).

Jenkins is now over seventy years old and retired. However, he and a friend recently took an extended fall backpacking trip along the Pacific Crest Trail. On their first night out, several miles north of Snoqualmie Pass, they ran into bad weather and had to camp in their tent in a snowstorm. They were well supplied with the latest lightweight equipment, but it was nonetheless one of the most miserable nights either of them had ever put in out in the Cascades.

Someone had pulled a practical joke by changing some signs at an earlier trail junction. After following what they thought was the right trail for several miles, they found themselves in the wrong drainage and had to backtrack. By then it was dark. They had to camp on a high, exposed ridge in an unseasonal snowstorm with a strong wind. Both Jenkins and his companion, an experienced outdoorsman in his mid-fifties, felt it was a tough situation. They had to hike through several miles of snow on the trail before getting below snowline into more comfortable surroundings. Cascade weather is as capricious as ever and can cause problems even for the experienced.

Over two decades after Jenkins did most of his on-the-spot learning of the ways of the wilderness, another man found nature still reigning supreme over the winter landscape in the Cascades. Like Jenkins, he had to draw on his own resources for survival. His experience prompted the founding of the Central Washington Mountain Rescue Unit, which has since rescued many an injured and stranded recreationist from the back country near Snoqualmie Pass and elsewhere in the region.

The story began at Fort Bragg, North Carolina, in 1955. Sergeant John Horan was planning to meet his wife and sons in Seattle, on their arrival from Japan. He hitchhiked across the country in military aircraft, carrying a Christmas present — a necklace — in his uniform pocket for his wife, Teruko. At Moses Lake, Washington, he got on a plane bound for Bellingham. High above the Snoqualmie Pass Highway, the airplane flew into a blizzard and the wings began to ice up. The engine and radio quit.

The pilot ordered Sergeant Horan and the two crewmen to bail out as the out-of-control airplane rapidly lost altitude. The sergeant was closest to the door, so he went first. The pilot regained control before anyone else could bail out and headed back to Moses Lake.

The spot where Horan bailed out was near an airplane radio marker, but because the plane's radio had failed, the crew could not pinpoint the location exactly. As it turned out, though, Horan had parachuted on the west edge of the area the crew marked out for the search.

Sergeant Horan's ordeal in the winter Cascades began on December 19, a snowy Sunday afternoon. He knew only that he was somewhere in the mountains of Washington. He landed waist-deep in seven-foot drifts on the backside (as seen from the highway) of Mount Margaret along Thetis Creek, which flows into Lake Kachess.

The plucky paratrooper had gone through survival training, and that knowledge saved his life during the next few days. First, he disentangled himself from the chute straps, then made a tent from the chute. He was wearing only his dress uniform — slight protection from the fifteen-below-zero temperature. He jumped around inside the chute for a couple of hours, then realized he would die if he stayed there, so he began wallowing through the snow, following the creek downstream for about six miles. He found a summer resort at Lake Kachess and broke a window of a locked cabin to get in. Inside he found some cocoa plus matches and wood for a fire.

In the meantime, civilians and military had launched a search. Ironically, the owner of the cabin that Horan had found — Stan Thomas of Ellensburg — had originally planned to visit the cabin that day to shovel snow from the roof. He was told, however, that his services were needed north of Cle Elum for the search for Horan and he ended up driving a snowmobile on a futile effort to find the missing sergeant.

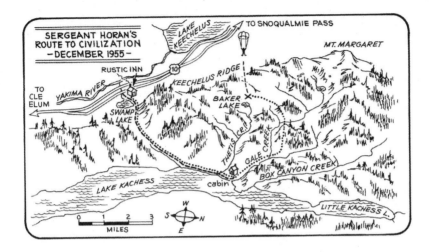

SERGEANT HORAN'S
ROUTE TO CIVILIZATION
—DECEMBER 1955—

At least one man in all those hundreds of square miles of forest had heard the plane having trouble as it flew over. Frank Brozovich, trapping for furs about a mile below Rustic Inn, heard the engine cut out and start up again. When he learned a man had bailed out and was missing, he contacted a deputy sheriff. The trapper and his partner, Vinko Kauzlarich, as well as two deputies, searched a wide area below the highway and Rustic Inn, but found nothing.

In the cabin, about five miles from Rustic Inn, Horan was busy figuring out how to escape the winter wilderness. The six-mile hike to the cabin Sunday night had left him with badly frost-bitten feet, which were swollen and blistered, but he did not spend much time resting. He tried making some skis out of cedar shakes from the roof, but he walked only 500 feet before they fell apart and he had to return to the cabin.

By Tuesday, his feet had swollen so much he could not get his shoes on, so he wrapped his feet with what he could find: pieces of inner tube and parts of a bedspread. He had heard sounds from the highway and passing trains to the south, so he started out once more. Once again, his improvised footgear did not hold up, and he returned to the cabin to avoid being caught in the woods after dark.

At this point, more than seventy-five searchers were involved. The Army, Air Force, and civilian personnel under the Kittitas County Sheriff had divided into three teams and were combing the hills north and east of Cle Elum. Local searchers came from Cle Elum, Ellensburg, Wenatchee, and Yakima. Someone thought he saw a bonfire on Mission Peak in the mountains between Wenatchee and Ellensburg, and a search force was sent in that direction. Back at Snoqualmie Pass, the two trappers and deputies were preparing to launch a search on Wednesday to the north of Rustic Inn, toward the vicinity where Horan was busy surviving.

The storm continued, so no airplanes could join the search. Each day, news stories originating in Cle Elum and Ellensburg were being filed on the wire services. It was the Christmas story of the decade. No one, especially the lost man's wife and mother, wanted to believe he was dead.

On Wednesday, Horan prepared himself for his supreme effort. He tore the metal shelves out of the cabin's icebox and began to fashion a makeshift pair of snowshoes. Using his parachute straps for bindings, he felt the idea might work, even though he had to slit his boots open to get his swollen, frozen feet inside.

He crawled out the cabin window — the door was still locked — put on the snowshoes, and bade goodbye to the cabin. This time, he would make it, or not, but he would not be back. The day was beginning to fade when he finally struggled the last of the five miles to the highway and tumbled down the snowbank onto the roadway just east of Rustic Inn.

Two employees of the inn — Paul Hays and Kelly Page — were the first to find him. They took him to the inn, cut the refrigerator shelves from his feet, removed his wet clothing, and got some hot broth and tea into him, followed by light food. He rested in bed in one of the inn's rooms as reporters and photographers swarmed in. That evening, Horan watched on television as his wife was told of his survival. The country rejoiced; many of the tired searchers wept with relief at the news. It would be a happy Christmas.

The Central Washington Mountain Rescue Unit was formed during a "critique" of the rescue operation right after Horan's ordeal. Whenever someone is lost or injured in the mountains, members of the voluntary organization come from Ellensburg, Wenatchee, and Yakima. Over the years, they have saved numerous lives.

9

Skiing

The factor that once was the greatest barrier to using the natural route through Snoqualmie Pass is now the very thing that attracts several million skiers annually to the summit area — all that snow. The area also has a relatively mild maritime climate and is within an hour's drive of a heavy-population area. Snoqualmie Pass is the country's only complex of ski areas of its size that is serviced by a multi-lane, interstate highway.

Most people mark the mid-1930s as the beginning of recreational skiing in the Northwest. It has an even earlier history in a relatively small, but important, coal-mining community just twenty-five miles east of Snoqualmie Pass, at Cle Elum. According to John "Syke" Bresko, a native of Cle Elum and the driving force behind skiing in the Northwest, Cle Elum had the first organized skiing west of Denver, although the sport on a highly informal level can be traced to the old California gold camps along the Feather River.

For Bresko, skiing began in 1920. Russ Connell, a trapper, convinced him to make a pair of skis from hickory wood that came from the Midwest. They got several other Cle Elum residents interested, including Jake Bizyack, Al Schober, Harry Parker, Fred Manley, John Koester, and Charlie Henry. At the time, they had only two pairs of skis among them, but by the end of that winter there were thirty-six skiers, and about half of them had skis.

Bresko served as president of the Cle Elum Ski Club for ten years, and during that time Cle Elum was a skier's paradise. The community sponsored numerous events, and chartered trains came from Puget Sound and Yakima to see and take part in the races, ski jumps, and special contests. No one who attended those tournaments in the 1920s and early 1930s is likely to forget Bresko's distinctive, baritone voice, booming over the whole course as he announced the events.

Volunteer winter sports enthusiasts from Cle Elum built a ski jump on the backside of a ridge north of the mining town. Even with the free labor, it cost $5,000. The Northern Pacific Railroad provided a tramway through a mine shaft to get near the ski jump. The fans poured into town on the Northern Pacific, were taken by truck to board mine cars, hauled by hoist to the mine shaft, and then had a twenty-minute walk to the ski hill. Other fans arrived in sleds pulled overland by large tractors. Bresko estimated the attendance in 1931 at more than 8,000. In addition to a two-story lodge, there was a long shed, 12 feet by 100 feet, with tables and six stoves, where volunteers helped prepare and serve soup and other food.

The Cle Elum ski tournaments were definitely a spectator sport. Before his death in 1978, Bresko talked about the old days: "Thousands came to the tournaments. The Friday-Saturday annual events included a dance, banquet, and trophy presentation, as well as the daytime competition. We had a lot of contests and events such as Rocky Run, Camel's Hump, Shoot the Chute, Devil's Dive, and Hell's Dive, which I dreamed up. We'd have 100 to 400 people on the ski hill every weekend through the winter. The big-time skiers didn't have a chance in

Newspaper photo of the Cle Elum ski jump, about 1931.

Ellensburg Library collection

these special events. The locals had been practicing all winter in anticipation of the mid-February show."

The tournaments expanded in 1923 and for the next eleven years were the high point of the winter season in Cle Elum. According to Bresko, they had seven ski jumpers that year from throughout the state, including Carl Solberg, a famous Norwegian skier who was living in Cle Elum at the time.

Cle Elum elected a royal court to preside over the ski tournaments each year, and the girls and chaperones traveled to other budding ski centers in Oregon and Washington. Bresko and the others who designed the Cle Elum ski jump and hill were called upon to be consultants for other communities that began to take an interest in ski tournaments.

The largest ski crowds Cle Elum had were in 1931, the first year Snoqualmie Pass was kept open all winter by the Highway Department, and those living on Puget Sound could drive through the pass rather than take the train. Though still a spectator sport, "Ski Mania" had struck in the Cascades. Following the Cle Elum tournament in February came the Snoqualmie Summit Ski Meet, with its ten-mile cross-country ski race to Source Lake. Spectators had to walk one and one-quarter miles to the ski hill where jumps were held, but they didn't mind at all.

The Depression and the opening of the pass to motor cars and busses all winter meant that Snoqualmie Pass itself, being closer to the larger population centers of Puget Sound, became the logical focal point for ski competition. By 1934, the Cle Elum tournaments ground to a halt.

Bresko had to drop his plans for a big ski development that included provisions for an aerial tramway. The old Northwest Improvement Company of Northern Pacific was prepared to install the tramway to develop more ski passenger travel on the railroad, but the dream never became a reality.

Bresko had another dream that never developed: "In 1924, I could have bought the government land at Snoqualmie Summit for just $2.85 an acre. I was really banking on the development of that area for winter sports. But my banker wouldn't advance the money; he claimed the lack of transportation would hold it all back. Just look at that Snoqualmie area now."

Today there are four ski areas within two miles of the pass with a total of fifty-nine lifts and tows — twenty-two chair lifts, three poma lifts, and thirty-four rope tows.

While Bresko was promoting recreational skiing on the east side of Snoqualmie Pass, The Mountaineers, a Seattle-based outdoor club, were getting established on the west side. They had been looking for a favorable mountain area in which to locate a lodge similar to the chalets that some Mountaineers had observed while traveling in the European Alps. They selected Snoqualmie Pass due to its year-round access via railroad, as well as its proximity to a car road (although the car road did not stay open for winter travel until the early 1930s). The lodge was completed in the fall of 1914. It was built on a knoll just two miles southwest of the pass, near the Cascade divide and 500 feet above Rockdale station, on the spot that is now the west portal of the Milwaukee Railroad tunnel. It was reached by a steep one-and-one-half-mile hiking trail from Rockdale.

Except for the logs cut on the building site, all materials had to be hauled up the trail from the railroad by horse or backpack. In the early days, snowshoeing was the favorite winter sport, but by 1920, skiing had become highly popular at the lodge. There were cross-country tours and races held on trails built by The Mountaineers, branching out from the homey log stucture. Working on their own and with the Forest Service, Mountaineers volunteers built trails out to several high lakes and peaks in the area.

The lodge was operated primarily as a climbing center for thirty years until it burned in 1944. However, during the years it was used, it spawned the building of another Mountaineers lodge on the east side of the pass; Meany Hut was built in 1928 due to the great popularity of skiing. It was built near Martin — or Tunnel City, which is the east portal of the Northern Pacific tunnel at Stampede Pass. In 1930, three-man-team events known as the Ski Patrol races were run over an eighteen-mile course to Meany Hut, beginning at the old Snoqualmie Lodge above Rockdale. The race could take anywhere from five hours to two days, depending on weather and snow conditions.

Today, neither Rockdale nor Martin exists as a railway station and the trains no longer make stops in the mountains to let off or pick up skiers and climbers. The Snoqualmie Pass Highway now offers year-round access to and from Seattle and mass downhill skiing at large, nearby resorts has replaced individual or team ski events. Both Meany Hut and The Mountaineers' new Snoqualmie Lodge, built in 1948 at the pass, have rope tows and offer Club members a place to stay with good skiing at hand.

Seattle Ski Club Lodge at Snoqualmie Pass, in the 1930s.

During those years when the railroad provided the best transportation through Snoqualmie Pass, the Milwaukee Railroad, with cooperation from the *Seattle Times* ski school, owned and operated a ski area known as the Snoqualmie Ski Bowl. The railroad began running special trains for skiers to the area in the late 1930s. The Snoqualmie Ski Bowl was located near the eastern portal of Snoqualmie tunnel. Its Class A jumping hill, where national jumps were held, is still visible east of present-day Hyak Hill.

It was popular to ride ski trains from Seattle, but when World War II broke out, the ski trains had to be cancelled. The ski area was shut down during the war, and when it reopened in 1946, the name was changed to the Milwaukee Ski Bowl. In December 1949, the Ski Bowl lodge burned down, the facilities were closed, and the area adjacent to where the jumps were, was sold. The area was later operated as Hyak Ski Area for a number of years and then as Mount Hyak.

In June, 1981, the bankrupt Hyak Skiing Corp. was sold at auction to lone bidder Safeco Credit Co., Inc., Hyak's major creditor. At that time, a Safeco official stated that the company planned to resell Hyak and that interested parties were considering developing the property into a year-round resort.

Webb Moffatt, owner of Snoqualmie Summit Ski Area and Ski Acres, is one of the pioneers of the skiing industry at Snoqual-

mie Pass. He arrived in 1937, in the days when Snoqualmie
Summit was still run by the Seattle Parks Department. It is today
all Forest Service land, except a section that belongs to Burlington Northern and a forty-acre piece Moffatt bought from the
Seattle Ski Club, which had been there since 1929. A photo that
he has from the first season of the old Summit Inn, shows a sign
on the building saying "500 yards Ski Lift Government Hill. All
Day Rates 50¢, 75¢ and $1.00."

  After the federal government formed the Civilian Conserva-
tion Corps (CCC) in 1933, the Seattle Park Board used a CCC
team to clear a patch of open area for a ski run. Moffatt re-

minisces, "Everything else up here was covered with dense trees. They were all over-age trees when we began clearing. You couldn't even sell the timber in those days. We had to cut it down and burn it. It wasn't until the war came along that there was a demand for pulp and they could sell the timber. When we finally cleared the hill for the chairlift, we sold the timber for a dollar a thousand. Now it's selling for $80 to $100. And they're making two-by-fours out of it and anything they can get."

The Seattle Park Board apparently got the original permit for the area from the Forest Service and operated it as a recreation area out of Seattle. About 1939, Seattle citizens complained that

Snoqualmie Summit Ski Area in 1937, before the slopes were "groomed" of trees.

Courtesy of Webb Moffatt

Main hill and rope tows of Summit Ski Area after the first major clearing, 1945.

the city should not be supporting a park so many miles away, and the permit was transferred to Ski Lifts, Incorporated — Webb Moffatt's employer.

After graduating from college as a civil engineer and finding no jobs available in the depression years, Moffatt had visited Seattle once and returned to pump gas. In 1937, he was fired, about which he comments, "They say your opportunities are sometimes made for you — or in spite of you." He read in the Sunday supplement of the *New York Times* about an endless rope device recently put up in Vermont to haul skiers up a hill. He thought the idea would work well in the Cascades so he started going around to Mount Rainier, Snoqualmie, and Mount Baker ski areas. Everybody said, "That's a great idea, but we've just signed a contract with Chauncy Griggs from Tacoma, called Ski Lifts, Incorporated."

Moffatt figured he might as well join them, so he talked himself into a job with Ski Lifts. Coworker Jim Parker had been involved with an early rope tow in the East, and the two men put up tows at Snoqualmie, Mount Rainier, and Mount Baker. Moffatt was earning $150 a month when there was business, but he had just been married, and he had to get a job at the Bremerton Navy Yard to make ends meet. He made a deal with Griggs that he would run Snoqualmie for $10 a weekend plus ten percent of the gross.

When the war came, Mount Rainier was closed to visitors and set aside for training mountain troops. Mount Baker was also closed. Griggs tried to sell the business but could not find a buyer. Together with a friend, Rance Morris, Moffatt raised $3,500 and bought Mount Rainer, Mount Baker, and Snoqualmie ski areas for that amount. In Rainier's last year of operation, 1941, it had grossed $28,000; Snoqualmie had made only $1,500 that year. Wartime gas rationing turned out well for Moffatt. People had only five gallons a week, but they wanted to ski anyway, so they pooled their rations and went to Snoqualmie. During the first year of business under the new owners, Snoqualmie grossed $800; the second, $1,600; then $3,200.

Mount Rainier, Mount Baker, and Stevens Pass ski areas had also been closed during the war, but they reopened after it, and Snoqualmie continued to operate. According to an article in a 1949 Ellensburg newspaper, Kittitas County led the state of Washington in ski areas, and six of the eight areas listed were near Snoqualmie Pass. By then, Moffatt had sold Mount Rainier and Mount Baker ski areas and was concentrating on Snoqualmie. For a brief time — 1943 to 1944 — he and his partner had tried rope tows at Blewett Pass but could not attract big enough crowds from the Ellensburg area, and then the Highway Department moved the mountain highway route from Blewett to Swauk Pass.

There was a real influx of skiers to the Snoqualmie area after the war. "We were the first in the country to put in night lighting," Moffatt remembers. "We did it so our employees would have a chance to ski, but it caught on so well with the customers, they began to enjoy it too. When the war was over, there was a lot of degaussing tape left over — big, heavy wire that was put around ships to counteract minefields. We got a lot of that and strung it around the surface of our ski area and put up service-station lights. That was 1945." Now, night skiing is a major part of the skiing business. Moffatt believes it is better at night than at day most of the time because the skier can see "every hump and bump."

Moffatt believes the biggest impetus to the expansion of skiing in the area has been stretchpants and chairlifts. "Stretchpants added fashion to skiing. People used to wear whatever they had — hiking boots, riding pants, anything. Chairlifts really came into their own in the '60s. That's when Alpental, Crystal Mountain, and Mission Ridge developed. We put in our first chair in 1954 — it's our Thunderbird chairlift and is still a favorite. We put in our Thunderbird Restaurant, about a thousand feet above Snoqualmie Pass, in 1955, and for several years ran the chair up to it during the summer, until the novelty wore off. It's open during the winter season now."

Attitudes toward the sport have changed, too. Moffatt explained that in the beginning skiing was mainly a spectator sport. As it developed, however, everyone wanted to ski. In the early days of Snoqualmie Summit Ski Area, the Seattle Ski Club had jumps on Beaver Lake Hill, and 2,000 people would show up to watch the jumps. They had to hike all the way up by foot on a path through the trees. The area was not even cleared yet. But after people got interested in skiing, they wouldn't go out of their way to watch a jump. They preferred to be skiing downhill themselves.

Another boost to the ski industry in Washington was the ski schools, for which Moffatt credits the Seattle newspapers. Ski schools at the Milwaukee Bowl were first offered through the *Seattle Times*, and when that program proved successful, the *Seattle Post-Intelligencer* started a free ski school with buses. As the programs became too popular for the papers alone to handle, the school districts and numerous other organizations got involved.

Ironic as it may seem, Moffatt does not ski very often anymore. "You don't get much chance when there's that much business to take care of and about 250 employees up here during peak season," he says. "When youngsters come to me asking to work here, I often ask them why. They usually say, 'Because I love to ski so much.' So I tell them that's just like the bartender who tells me he loves to tend bars because he likes to drink so much."

Ray Tanner, former owner of Ski Acres, is another pioneer of the Snoqualmie Pass ski industry, but he did not start out to go into the skiing business. He and his wife came to Snoqualmie Pass to find a piece of land where they could build a cabin for their two children. One thing led to another; they had the opportunity to buy the land now occupied by Ski Acres, so they did. It was about 350 acres, although the ski area is smaller now.

When Ski Acres started business in the fall of 1948, Snoqualmie Pass, the Hyak Ski Bowl, Stevens Pass, and Mount Rainier at Paradise were all in operation. Ski Acres, barely on the east side

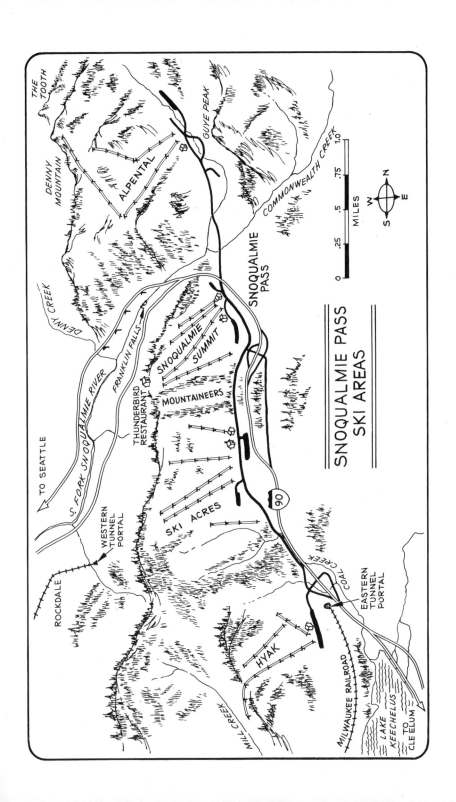

SNOQUALMIE PASS
SKI AREAS

of Snoqualmie Pass, began with a single chair and two double rope tows. At first, the Tanners thought they were fortunate to have 200 or 300 people on the hill at one time, and a ski school on weekends drew between 1,200 and 1,400 people. Today, in the midst of ski season, they have from 6,000 to 7,000 people in a day.

When Ski Acres first opened, Tanner saw a great deal of "Army reject skis or Army surplus skis. They were hickory painted white, and they ran around seven feet in length. Skiers used to cut the tail end off of them."

Tanner agrees with Moffatt that the ski business in the Northwest has developed from ski schools to a large degree. He says, "All the ski area operators have gone out and helped work with the school districts to form ski schools within school districts that are run by the PTA or a committee of some sort. The Northwest has been particularly good at increasing the number of people coming to the ski areas." This increase has occurred in spite of

Milwaukee Ski Bowl, late 1930s.

A series of modern chairlifts now take skiers to tops of runs at the Summit Ski Area.

rising gasoline costs, and Tanner now estimates that there are 4,000 to 5,000 ski instructors in the Northwest, calling it the biggest complex of teaching in the world. "Skiing in the Northwest has helped the whole industry," he says. "The increase per year is about fifteen percent or better."

After ski schools and ski instructing, Tanner credits snow-grooming equipment for the increase in the sport's popularity. Each area has its own equipment designed for its own kind of snow. There is a general design, but every area modifies it because the snow can be completely different from one ski area to another.

At Ski Acres, they started out manicuring the hill by hand and foot, sidestepping up it. Tanner says, "We tried to get a whole bunch of kids to go up on the lift and sidestep down in a line, but it wasn't too practical — people really didn't go for it." They started using grooming equipment about fifteen years ago and then improved on it. The most recent machine they bought cost $55,000. In all, they have eight snow-grooming machines and a couple of graders, snow blowers, and trucks. They clean their parking lots and keep the road shoulders clean. The Highway Department plows out the road. Ski Acres can accommodate 3,000 cars and 150 buses, plus room for campers and trailers — a long step from the days of 200 people at a time.

Tanner feels that the most important help to the skiing industry at Snoqualmie Pass is its proximity to a big metropolitan area and the multi-lane highway that comes through. "Also," he says, "we don't have too cold weather here, and the night skiing has been fantastic — it's a good fifty percent of our business. You can ski everything we've got up here at nighttime, and we run all our equipment at night. Back East, it gets too cold at night and skiers can't stand it. Night business is like having a whole other day to run."

Snoqualmie Pass saw the addition of yet another ski area with the opening of Alpental during the 1967-68 ski season. Located two miles north of the summit on Alpental Road, the area was originally started by a partnership of Tacoma businessmen. In 1977, it was purchased by Westours, a Seattle-based Alaska tour operator. The area is designed for the intermediate and advanced skier.

The skiing business has been an intimate part of the changing character of the pass and the highway for years — so much so that for a time it seems that the skiing business controlled the highway. An environmental impact statement, released in 1970 and titled *Description of the Highway Improvements and its Surroundings*, states, "Highway and skier oriented businesses crowded along its shoulders, eager to attract the business of highway travelers. The result was a virtual takeover of the highway's right of way by summit visitors. Pedestrians strolled casually across the four-lane highway and incidents of illegal or highly dangerous stopping, turning, and parking were rampant. The accident rate soared, and the problems of snow removal from the highway without blocking adjacent businesses became almost insurmountable. Eventually, this congestion spelled the early demise of the highway for its intended purpose. It was then necessary to bypass the entire strip with another highway alignment."

Probably not many of the early skiing enthusiasts foresaw the day when the sport could be said to have overrun the highway itself. Even now it is hard to identify future changes, but with parking for more than 20,000 vehicles predicted for the summit ski areas by 1986, it is evident that the highway will continue to change.

10

Controlling the Traffic

Until 1921, law and order along the Snoqualmie Pass Highway was in the hands of the local sheriffs of King and Kittitas counties. Effective June 8 of that year, the State Legislature created the Highway Patrol, later renamed the Washington State Patrol. The original patrol force was made up of six men who covered the entire state, working either out of their own homes or out of the office of whatever sheriff or police chief was nearby. The patrolmen were issued a cap, badge, emblem, and gun, but there were no uniforms until 1925.

Communication was by mail or telephone until the mid-1930s, when the first radio communications came. From 1922 to around 1930, patrolmen used a stopwatch by the side of the road to catch speeders by clocking them between two points. Much of the road over Snoqualmie Pass was gravel until the late 1920s, when oil was first applied to either end to hold the dust down. Although the speed for cars was raised from thirty to forty miles an hour in 1927, there were still few stretches on that road where top speed could be enjoyed.

The State Patrol used motorcycles with sidecars until 1931. That year, the first panel truck in the state was put into use on Snoqualmie Pass — a combination mobile jail, patrol car, and ambulance. As the patrolmen drove back and forth over the route at night, a small, constantly blinking red light mounted over the vehicle identified it as an official patrol car that would provide aid to motorists in trouble. The old panel vehicles were later replaced by coupes, then by four-door sedans about 1947.

During the 1950s and 1960s, there was a Snoqualmie Pass Washington State Patrol Detachment office in the highway building on the summit. With the building of new highway maintenance facilities at Hyak, the State Patrol office was phased out. Now patrols over the summit come from the North Bend and Cle Elum offices, with Ellensburg administering the east side and North Bend administering the west. If there is a storm and the number of accidents is rising, both detachments dispatch several patrol units to the area, provided there are no problems elsewhere.

While the modern-day trooper is better equipped than the early-day counterpart, patrolling Snoqualmie Pass still offers plenty of challenge. The mountain road is subject to more than the usual number of road hazards because it traverses mountains and the headwaters of two of the state's major river systems. There have been natural disasters — rockslides, avalanches, floods, fires — that have threatened motorist safety more than once, as well as the winter blizzards that have either snarled traffic or shut down the route for several days at a time.

The State Patrol now has an emergency four-wheel-drive vehicle patrolling the pass on either side of the summit. It is a power wagon equipped with a winch, ropes, special rescue equipment, and first-aid gear. The vehicle operates in Snoqualmie Pass during the winter and along Washington's ocean beaches during the summer to improve public safety in both areas.

Glen Cramer, whose beat extends from Ellensburg to Snoqualmie Summit, is one of several troopers who patrol the pass. The following description of his work day should reveal the hazards of Snoqualmie Pass travel, as well as precautions to be taken by today's motorist.

Cramer drives an average of 200 miles a day on patrol — 3,000 to 4,000 miles a month. He must be always on the alert for anything unusual that attracts attention, such as erratic driving caused by too much alcohol or too little sleep. He likes to drive over his complete route the first thing when he comes on duty — unless something else comes up — to learn the feel of the road and the weather and driving conditions. There's plenty of opportunity to make contact with the public right off, such as a motorist with engine trouble or a violator. For example, if he spots a pickup in the eastbound lanes with only one headlight working, he makes a U-turn and quickly pulls the truck over. He gives the driver a verbal warning and sends him on his way. By giving this warning early enough in the afternoon, Cramer

makes sure that the driver can stop at a garage and get the
headlight fixed before dark, thereby cutting down on accident
potential.

Because he drives the pass regularly and observes weather
conditions, Cramer can almost predict when and where accidents
are likely to happen. He explains, "The usual cause of the accidents is people driving too fast for conditions or not having
proper winter driving equipment. Quite often people begin to
have problems on banked icy curves that come right after a fairly
long, level stretch of road. Especially when it's just beginning to
snow — they come along and go into the curve a little too fast
and plow into the snowbank." Tracks leading off into the snowy
median strip will attest to the truth of his statement.

Freeway driving on Snoqualmie Pass in the winter is far different from in the summer or from freeway driving in the lowlands of Puget Sound. Quite often accidents happen as a result
of cars driving in clusters, especially during a snowstorm. If just
one car without snow tires starts to skid or spin out, there is
nowhere for the other drivers to go — no escape — as the snow is
banked up high on either side. Cramer suggests that when driving during the snow months, "It's better to let others pass
and not try to keep the same pace as everyone else. Try to leave
plenty of room."

Another trouble spot is at exits from the freeway on to snowy
roads. Cramer explains, "It takes all the Highway Department's
efforts during a storm or when conditions are icy just to keep
the traffic moving through the pass, and sometimes exits are not
sanded quite as well as the main traffic lanes. It is easier to slow
down before reaching the exit ramp — rather than trying to slow
down after getting on it, finding that it is super slick, and ending
up upside down, in a snowbank or in a collision with someone
else."

Radio communications are vital to keeping the traffic moving
through Snoqualmie Pass. In some cases, CB radio reports on
accidents have helped, but these descriptions of accident locations are often unreliable. Cramer notes, "The best way for a
motorist to identify the location of an accident is to use the last
overpass number or milepost marker before the accident scene."

When Cramer goes to the scene of an accident, he usually does
not use his flashing lights. He explains, "People see me coming
up behind them with the lights on, slow down, and pull over too

fast — thinking the lights are for them — and wind up in the snowbank. I just want to drive to the scene as rapidly as possible, safely, so I don't wind up in an accident myself."

One accident that occurred just east of the summit exemplifies the conditions the State Patrol is up against. Descending Hyak Hill in response to a call, Cramer rounded a curve just below Ski Acres, and there was a big semi-truck that had skidded, slid backwards, and was headed uphill blocking the outside lane. The cab was bent. Just before the curve, a State Highway Department pickup was parked, and flares had been set out to warn other motorists to pull into the inside lane and to tell them there had been an accident.

It was now dark and a heavy snowstorm was in progress. Big, wet flakes were coming down and the road had a glaze. Cars were still coming by too fast. Cramer pulled in front of the truck in order to avoid being involved in a collision in case anyone were to slide into the accident scene. The truck had ended up facing the wrong way on a banked curve, and until it was towed out of the way, it was a traffic hazard. Cramer checked that sufficient flares were out because other drivers could not see the truck until they had rounded the bend. Many were slow to interpret the warning flares and stayed in the outside lane until the last minute. Snow was banked about four feet high on each side of the two eastbound lanes.

The truck driver, shivering with cold and shock, did not want to leave his vehicle. After ascertaining that the truck was not loaded, Cramer coaxed the driver into the back of the patrol car and applied minor first aid to abrasions on the driver's arm and leg. (Each trooper has cardio-pulmonary resuscitation training and other first-aid training so he can give immediate, possibly life-saving, aid to accident victims. Because hazardous chemicals cross the pass, patrolmen also receive considerable instruction about the main chemicals that are commercially hauled and about what to do in case of accident or spillage. If the wrecked truck had been loaded, Cramer would have immediately asked to see the bill of lading to determine whether there would be any problem from spilled chemicals. If necessary, he could have ordered the highway sealed off. If it had looked as if any material might seep into nearby water channels, he would have notified the Department of Ecology to supervise mop-up operations and prevent contamination of downstream communities.)

Cramer stood beside the patrol car talking through his open window into his radio microphone to advise North Bend of the status of the situation, and he suddenly yelped and leaped behind the car. Simultaneously there was an echoing boom as another truck rounded the banked curve and slid into the wrecked truck, ricocheting on by. It just missed the patrol car. Cramer was immediately back on his radio requesting more traffic control at the east summit interchange to slow people down before anything else happened.

The tow truck soon arrived, and the ticklish operation of moving the first wrecked truck began. At the summit, the Highway Department shunted traffic into one lane while the patrol car and the tow truck hauling the disabled vehicle paraded against traffic to the summit and got off the freeway and out of a dangerous situation. Once off the freeway, the trucker got into the tow truck to head back to Cle Elum.

Snowplowing operations are taken mostly for granted by winter travelers crossing Snoqualmie Pass, but to clear the forty-five feet of annual snowfall — sometimes falling at the rate of a foot an hour — the Highway Department requires a small army of skilled people using expensive equipment under the worst possible conditions. Snow and ice control costs over $20,000 a mile each year in that area — a great percentage of the total maintenance cost of the highway.

Under moderate snowfall conditions, four lanes are patrolled by three plow-sander trucks traveling in a staggered platoon. With the lead truck crowding the centerline, these three plows can clear the two lanes in the direction they are traveling, rolling the snow onto the shoulder. On the return trip, they clear the opposing lanes. Their second trip in each direction crowds the right-hand shoulder, moving the snow farther to the right and packing it into the ditch in as high a windrow as possible. During the process, the last truck is applying sand or sand and salt, and the trucks rotate positions within the platoon as their sand supply is depleted. As this accumulated snow builds up on the shoulders, it rapidly fills up the limited storage area available there. Depending on the intensity of snowfall, this may take several days or several hours. Either way, when the shoulders can no longer store additional snow, power-driven rotary snowplows are moved in, which pick up the accumulated snow from the shoulder and throw it a greater distance off the roadbed. Road graders are regularly used to keep the compacted snow on the roadway smooth and level.

Eventually, snow that has been blown to the uphill side accumulates enough depth that it tends to slide back down onto the roadway, and it is necessary to come back and blow that snow all the way across four lanes to the downhill side. This is a slow, inefficient operation — which is why this method is avoided when possible — because a considerable curtain of snow is created during the blowing process. The curtain so impairs visibility that traffic must be stopped in both directions, and enough snow drops onto the roadway that it must be plowed. Every effort is made to do this type of work late at night when traffic is light, but the weather does not always cooperate.

How different modern snow removal methods are from those in the early part of the century. Some years the pass was closed five months or longer as there were no tools to remove it. In June 1917, an article in the weekly Cle Elum *Echo* told of a citizens' effort to open the pass:

Highway Department crews work to clear eastbound lane totally blocked by avalanche off Keechelus Ridge. For several hours, all traffic had to share the lanes under the adjacent snowshed.

Yvonne Prater photo

Chairman [of County Commissioners] McNeil offers in behalf
of Kittitas county to clean two and a half miles of snow if the citizens of Ellensburg, Cle Elum and Roslyn will take care of the remaining mile. A heavy grader will be taken to the pass at once and
put to work and Sunday the citizens of these towns are invited to
hie themselves mountainward with shovels.

It will be called a "snow line picnic." Everybody who can possibly
get away is asked to go. Several extra cars are to be provided here
in town for those who will go but have no means of getting there.

No stated hour for the whole bunch to leave has been set but
cars are urged to get up to the snow line just as early as possible.
Campfires will be built and a good time is surely in store for every
man and woman who goes — for the women are invited and are
very necessary to look after the commissary. County Engineer
Murray will direct the work. If everybody puts pep into this final
effort to unlock the Sunset highway to travel it will go through
with a rush and we shall soon see the cars pouring through town.

Those who drove the last car to cross the pass before winter
snows closed it, and the first car through the next spring, often
made front page news in those days.

Avalanche control is performed by the Washington State Department of Transportation with cooperation from the Forest
Service. When weather indicates avalanche danger, recoilless
rifles are transported to stationary mounts in the mountains and
rocket-type shells carrying two pounds of high explosives are
fired at the start zone of the avalanche in order to trigger the
slide during a period of little danger. This method has been use-
ful in reducing avalanche-related injuries, but it is potentially
very hazardous to snowshoers and cross-country skiers in the vicinity. For this reason, avalanche conditions should be checked
with the ski ranger at either Snoqualmie Summit, North Bend,
or Cle Elum before snowshoers or cross-country skiers venture
into the area.

Various other aids help today's motorist. At the North Bend
and West Ellensburg interchanges, signs indicate the current
road conditions in the pass. There is also a "SNO line" telephone
recording from the North Bend ranger district, updated four
times a day; it gets about 1.5 million calls in a season. Radio
transmitters in Cle Elum and North Bend allow an AM car radio
to pick up messages; highway signs tell the motorist when the
transmitter is in range — about one mile from either North Bend
or Cle Elum. In addition, large, lighted signs now warn the

Snow removal equipment is a common sight during winter months on this year-round highway.

motorist what type of traction devices are required or recommended.

Many people start from the warm Puget Sound side of the mountains with no preparation made or extra gear along in case winter driving conditions prevail. At any time of year, a full tank of gas is advisable when heading over Snoqualmie Pass, and in winter, snow tires, tire chains, a flashlight, and at least one wool blanket are important commodities.

In 1980, I-90 through Snoqualmie Pass was closed for one week for the first time in the history of the road due to an unusual "calamity closure" caused by the May 18 eruption of Mount St. Helens. Visibility was reduced to zero by the volcanic ashfall. The Department of Emergency Services in Olympia publishes a pamphlet, "Volcanic Ashfall," that explains the hazards of ashfall and recommends equipment to be carried "just in case." During ashfall, it explains, do not drive above fifteen miles per hour, change oil and oil filter every 100 miles or so in heavy dust (less than fifty feet visibility), and if car stalls, push it off the road and stay with it. Through the summer of 1980, it was common to see truckers and motorists routinely carrying "volcanic masks," dangling from their rear-view mirrors.

Afterword

The changes made over the years to accommodate more people on the route over Snoqualmie Pass have wiped out all but a few traces of the old road that has so much of our history worn into it. In 1965, the Boy Scouts, the Forest Service, and private land holders cooperated to preserve a one-mile section of the original wagon road/early car road that switchbacks down from the Snoqualmie Summit to Denny Creek. In 1969, this was entered onto the Washington State List of Historic Places and is now protected as a valuable historic resource.

Though blacktopped, the preserved route gives a good idea of what it was like to drive through a deep Puget Sound forest, and the traveler wishing to relive history can actually drive there. Along the way, there is a section a couple of miles long where one can hike the old wagon road. Cedar puncheon, where the old wagon road crossed wet places, is still visible. There is also a Model T water trough where car radiators were refilled on the steep grade.

The road winds up through a huge rockslide that closed the main highway for a whole summer in the early 1960s. While truck traffic was shunted over other passes, car traffic was allowed to use the historic route while the slide was cleared and the four-lane route repaired.

Other reminders of the old days, and of the sequence of names that have changed with the highway, also remain. In 1915, the Yellowstone Trail Association was incorporated with general offices in Aberdeen, South Dakota. A man named W. Warwick was hired by the organization to travel westward from Plymouth, Massachusetts, marking the road along the way to designate it as the Yellowstone Trail. Warwick worked across the country to about fifteen miles outside Seattle, but at that point there were no more funds available and the project was stopped. At the time, this route, which eventually crossed Snoqualmie Pass, was one of the few cohesive coast-to-coast routes in the country. It varied in width, sometimes narrowing to a single lane with turnouts. Western attractions were Glacier, Yellowstone, and Rainier national parks, plus the Rockies, Bitterroots, Cascades, and many historic places.

Not long ago, I was photographing foxgloves near Denny Creek and saw in my viewfinder a yellow and black circle with an arrow pointing in the direction of Yellowstone National Park. This survivor from Warwick's work had hardly faded over the years. It was painted on the receding wall of a rock overhang, and a fair amount of vegetation had grown up in front. Later I discovered that there is a gateway five miles outside Aberdeen in Ipswich, marking the beginning of the western section of the trail.

The Yellowstone Road (also known as the Red Trail) had two routes into Seattle. The first went from Fall City to the Redmond-Kirkland ferry across Lake Washington, the largest freshwater ferry on the West Coast, and the second branched around the north end of the lake through Woodinville and Bothell. There is still a section of the old brick Yellowstone Road, off the Redmond–Fall City highway near Redmond, that is entered on the National Register of Historic Places. It is a narrow, slightly curving, one-mile section, again marked with humps and hollows, some bricks missing and small plants growing between bricks here and there. In a rural setting, it is like a trip back to the 1930s.

The Serpentine Trail and Sunset Highway designations need no explanation. During the summer of 1978, I took Forest Service archaeologist Susan Carter over the existing remnant of cattle and military trail over Keechelus Ridge; later we walked on the Indian packer's/Hudson's Bay Company trail from Lake Keechelus to Cedar River Pass. The Forest Service is now documenting these areas and perhaps they too can be saved. Both are visible from today's freeway if you know where to look.

In 1978, I also climbed Tinkham Peak with Morris Jenkins. On the way we found the site of his Mirror Lake cabin, where there were parts of his old cookstove, the snowshoe bindings he made

The old and the new: foreground, main switchback west of the summit on the old highway, the route of the original wagon road; background, viaduct on the divided-lane highway near Denny Creek, opened 1981.

from boots, and some old bottles — all of which we left as we found them. From the top of Tinkham there is a panorama of lakes — Cottonwood, Mirror, Glasses, Lost, and Keechelus — as well as a view of I-90.

Later, the Monahan family, who owns the townsite and mill of Cabin Creek, helped me find other remnants of the old wagon road, including a camping area between Cabin Creek, and Lake Keechelus. There are puncheon and small cedar bridges still marking the route.

Snoqualmie Pass, the easiest and lowest route through the Cascade Mountain Range from the Columbia River to the forty-ninth parallel, is rich in history. It lacks only public awareness and appreciation. In being more aware of past events, landmarks, and the changes the area has experienced, perhaps we can consider more carefully what happens to Snoqualmie Pass in the future.

154

BIBLIOGRAPHY

I. Books and Reports

Avery, Mary. *A History of the Evergreen State.* Seattle, Wash.: University of Washington Press, 1965.

Bagley, Clarence B. *History of King County,* Vol. 1. Seattle, Wash.: S.J. Clarke Publishing Co., 1929.

Bancroft, Hubert. *Bancrofts Works,* Vol. 31. San Francisco, Calif.: History Company Publishers, 1890.

Brown, Joseph, Editor. *Valley of the Strong.* Yakima, Wash.: Westcoast Publishing Co., 1974.

Corliss, Margaret McKibben. *Fall City in the Valley of the Moon.* Snoqualmie, Wash.: Snoqualmie Valley Historical Society, 1972.

Craine, Bessie Wilson. *Squak Valley* (Issaquah). Issaquah, Wash.: Issaquah Historical Society, 1976.

Denny, Arthur A. *Pioneer Days on Puget Sound.* Seattle, Wash.: Alice Harriman Co., 1908.

Washington State Highway Department. *Description of the Highway Improvement and Its Surroundings.* April 4, 1970.

Fish, Edwards. *The Past at Present.* Kingsport, Tenn.: Kingsport Press, 1967.

Fleming, Edna. *Ah Kittitas!* Yakima, Wash.: Franklin Press, 1969.

Gallagher, Dale G., Editor. *The Snowy Torrents.* Alta, Colo.: U.S. Department of Agriculture, U.S. Forest Service, 1967.

Geology Department, University of Washington. *A Geologic Trip Along Snoqualmie, Swauk, and Stevens Pass Highways.* Olympia, Wash.: State Printing Plant, 1963.

Glauert, Earl, and Kunz, Merle, Editors. *The Kittitas Indians.* Ellensburg, Wash.: Ellensburg Library, 1972.

Glauert, Earl, and Kunz, Merle, Editors. *Kittitas Frontiersmen.* Ellensburg, Wash.: Ellensburg Library, 1976.

Grant, James, Editor. *History of Seattle.* New York, N.Y.: American Publishing and Engraving Co., 1891.

Helland, Maurice. *They Knew Our Valley.* Yakima, Wash.: author published, 1975.

Helland, Maurice. *Our Valley, Too.* Yakima, Wash.: author published, 1976.

Hill, Ada. *A History of the Snoqualmie Valley.* Snoqualmie, Wash.: Snoqualmie Valley Historical Society, 1970.

History Committee. *Our Snoqualmie Community 1855-1956.* Snoqualmie, Wash.: Community Development Program, 1955.

History Committee. *Operation Cooperation.* Cle Elum, Wash.: Community Development Study, 1955.

Hodges, L.K., Editor. *Mining in Eastern & Central Washington* (facsimile reproduction from the larger work, *Mining in the Pacific Northwest,* L.K. Hodges, Editor, published in 1897 by the *Seattle Post-Intelligencer*). Seattle: The Shorey Bookstore, 1970.

Hodges, L.K., Editor. *Mining in Western Washington* (facsimile reproduction from the larger work, *Mining in the Pacific Northwest,* L.K. Hodges, Editor, published in 1897 by the *Seattle Post-Intelligencer*). Seattle: The Shorey Bookstore, 1967.

Jackson, W. Turrentine. *Wagon Roads West.* Los Angeles, Calif.: University of California Press, 1952.

Jordan, Josee. *You're at Liberty Here–Mines and Miners of The Swauk.* Yakima,

Wash.: Franklin Press, 1967.

Kirk, Ruth, and Daugherty, Richard D. *Exploring Washington Archaeology.* Seattle, Wash.: University of Washington Press, 1978.

Lyman, W.D. *History of the Yakima Valley,* Vol. 1. S.J. Clarke Publishing Co. (location unknown), 1919.

McKee, Bates. *Cascadia–The Geologic Evolution of the Pacific Northwest.* New York, N.Y.: McGraw-Hill Book Co., 1972.

Majors, Harry M. *Exploring Washington.* Holland, Mich.: Van Winkle Publishing Co., 1975.

Newell, Gordon. *Westward to Alki.* Seattle, Wash.: Superior Publishing Co., 1977.

Oliphant, J. Orin. *On the Cattle Ranges of the Oregon Country.* Seattle, Wash.: University of Washington Press, 1968.

Operation Uplift. *Spawn of Coal Dust.* Roslyn, Wash.: Community Development Program, 1955.

Prosch, Thomas W. *David S. Maynard and Catherine T. Maynard.* Seattle, Wash.: Lowman and Hanford Publishers, 1906.

Ruffner, W.H. *A Report on Washington Territory.* New York, N.Y.: Seattle, Lakeshore & Eastern Railway, 1889.

Scofield, W.M. *Washington's Historical Markers.* Portland, Oreg.: Touchstone Press, 1967.

Shiach, William. *A History of Klickitat, Yakima and Kittitas Counties.* Chicago, Ill.: The Interstate Publishing Co., 1904.

Smith, Clareta O. *Campfires in the Valley.* Wenatchee, Wash.: Wenatchee World Publishers, 1976.

Snowden, Clinton A. *History of Washington,* Vol 4. New York, N.Y.: Century History Co., 1909.

Splawn, A.J. *Ka-Mi-Akin, The Last Hero of the Yakimas.* Caldwell, Idaho: Caxton Printers, 1917.

U.S. Government. *Reports of Explorations and Surveys from the Mississippi River to the Pacific Ocean,* Vol. 1. "Explorations and Surveys for the Pacific Railroad." Washington, D.C., 1855.

U.S. Works Progress Administration, Washington State. *As Told by the Pioneers,* Vol. 2. Federal Writer's Project, 1938.

Washington Department of Highways. *40 Years with the Washington Department of Highways.* Olympia, Wash.: Department of Highways, 1945.

Watt, Roberta Frye. *The Story of Seattle.* Seattle, Wash.: Lowman and Hanford Co., 1932.

Whitfield, William. *History of Snohomish County.* Chicago, Ill.: Pioneer Historical Publishing Co., 1926.

Winthrop, Theodore. *The Canoe and the Saddle.* Boston, Mass.: Ticknor and Fields, 1864.

II. Pamphlets

A Citizen's Guide to Redmond, Washington. League of Women Voters of Lake Washington East, 1975.

Facts About Cle Elum, Washington and the Scenic and Historic Upper Kittitas County. Cle Elum Chamber of Commerce (undated).

How to Prepare for and What to Do during a Volcanic Ashfall. Olympia, Wash.: Federal Emergency Management Agency with assistance of the Washington State

Department of Emergency Services, 1980.

King County, East Seattle's Next Door Neighbor: Bellevue, Bothell, Issaquah, Kirkland, North Bend, Redmond, Woodinville. Spokane, Wash.: Tourmap Co., 1979.

Military Forts That Guarded the Valley by Elva Bush Polley. Fall City, Wash.: Fall City Senior 4-H Girls, circa 1939.

Mohawk Hobbs Grade and Surface Guide: Yellowstone Trail, Seattle-Chicago. Akron, Ohio: Tourist Service Department of the Mohawk Rubber Co., 1926.

North Bend and the Snoqualmie Valley. North Bend (Wash.) Chamber of Commerce (undated).

Passage West. Forest Service, U.S. Dept. of Agriculture (undated).

Redmond, Wshington. Greater Redmond Chamber of Commerce, 1977.

See Surprising Washington. Pacific Northwest Bell Telephone Co., 1971.

Ski Acres and Snoqualmie Summit Are Now One, 1980.

Ski Washington State. Olympia Wash.: Dept. of Commerce and Economic Development, Travel Development Division, Oct. 1978.

Snoqualmie Falls. Bellevue, Wash.: Puget Power Co., circa 1975.

Snoqualmie Pass Wagon Road. Snoqualmie National Forest, U.S. Forest Service, circa 1970.

The Gilman Village Story. Gilman Village (undated).

The Memorial Arch at Ipswich, South Dakota. Ipswich, S. Dak.: Edmunds Historical Association, April 6, 1936.

The Race. Ford Motor Co. Archives. Polyprints, Inc.: San Francisco, Calif. (undated).

The Valley Historical Tours Snoqualmie Valley. North Bend, Wash.: Snoqualmie Valley Historical Society, 1976.

The Yellowstone Trail: A Good Road from Plymouth Rock to Puget Sound. Ipswich, S. Dak.: Yellowstone Highway Association, 1935.

Visit Historic Kirkland 1976. Kirkland, Wash.: Arline Ely and Associates, 1976.

Winter Recreational Parking Program. Olympia, Wash.: Washington State Parks (undated).

III. Magazine Articles

Brain, Eugene J. "Thorp, Washington." *The Coast,* May 1908.

Coleman, Edmund. "Puget Sound and the Northern Pacific Railroad." *Pacific Northwest Quarterly,* Vol. 3, 1932.

Edwards, G. Thomas. "Terminus Disease." *Pacific Northwest Quarterly,* October 1979.

"Fall City." *The Coast,* June 1909.

Hubbell, J.C. "Ellensburg, Washington." *The Coast,* May 1908.

Johnson, W.W. "Easton, Washington." *The Coast,* May 1908.

Kauffman, J.J. "Kittitas County, Washington." *The Coast,* May 1908.

Mires, Austin. "Early History of Kittitas County." *The Coast,* May 1908.

Moffett, Webb. "A Brief History of Skiing in the Northwest." *Puget Soundings Magazine,* December 1978.

Morley, Roberta Crisp. "Tree Stumps and Cattle Trails." *Washington Cattleman,* June 1970.

Mullen, Captain John. "From Walla Walla to San Francisco." *Oregon Historical Quarterly,* September 1903.

Overmeyer, Philip. "George B. McClellan and the Pacific Northwest." *Pacific Northwest Quarterly,* January 1941.

Perleur, Becky. "Thorps Tamed the Area." *Campus Crier* (Central Washington University), Spring Special, March 27, 1978.

Short, G.P. "Cle Elum, Washington." *The Coast,* May 1908.

IV. Newspaper Articles With Bi-lines

Anderson, Edward. "Century of Highway Progress Told by Local Road Leader." Ellensburg, Wash., *Daily Record,* July 6, 1953.

Bebermeyer, Ralph. "Road to Move Ipswich Arch." Aberdeen, S. Dak., *Aberdeen American News,* January 10, 1933.

Belanger, Herb. "Hikers Alert: Avalanche Danger Great in Springtime." *Seattle Times,* May 18, 1978.

Burns, Alma. "Arrival by Blacks in Roslyn Celebrated." Ellensburg, Wash., *Daily Record,* August 7, 1978.

Churchhill, Sam. "Sam's Valley." Yakima, Wash. *Herald-Republic,* February 3, 1973.

Conover, C.T. "Building the Road Across Snoqualmie Pass." *Seattle Times,* July 9, 1949.

Conover, C.T. "Seattleite's History of Building Snoqualmie Road." *Seattle Times,* August 6, 1961.

Conover, C.T. "When Cattle Walked Across Snoqualmie Pass to Seattle." *Seattle Times,* November 11, 1947.

Duncan, Don. "Best Gift Under the Tree; 2 Refrigerator Shelves Have Place of Honor." *Seattle Times,* December 24, 1980.

Falk, L.E. "Edmunds County Town Is Home of 1st U.S. Trail." Aberdeen, S. Dak., *Aberdeen American News,* January 3, 1932.

Fish, By. "Snoqualmie Jams Close to Tragedy." *Seattle Times,* December 19, 1968.

Glover, Darrell. "Kirkland Building Named." *Seattle Post-Intelligencer,* April 10, 1971.

Helland, Morie. "Yakimas Put Traders Courage to the Test." Yakima, Wash., *Herald-Republic,* January 12, 1975.

Johnson, Jim. "Fall City Centennial." *Seattle Times,* June 11, 1972.

Kramer, Stanley. "He's a Gravedigger, Black and Mayor." *Seattle Times,* August 13, 1978.

Kuo, Keming. "Trucks Wait for Passes to Open." *Seattle Times,* February 7, 1979.

Lane, Bob. "Group Steams Ahead to Fix up Old Snoqualmie Train Station." *Seattle Times,* November 24, 1975.

McDonald, Lucille. "Crossing Snoqualmie Pass Hasn't Always Been Easy." Bellevue, Wash., *Daily Journal American,* April 2, 1979.

McDonald, Lucille. "Snoqualmie Pass is 50 Years Old." *Seattle Times,* July 18, 1965.

McDonald, Lucille. "Whidbey Island Doctor Proposed Snoqualmie Road 100 Years Ago." *Seattle Times,* November 30, 1952.

McGiffin, Jim. "Cle Elum's John Bresko, a Western Ski Pioneer." Ellensburg, Wash., *Daily Record,* December 9, 1972.

McGiffin, Joy. "Black Pioneers Picnic Set for Roslyn." Ellensburg, Wash., *Daily Record,* July 29, 1981.

McGiffin, Joy. "Gravestones Spin Tale." Ellensburg, Wash., *Daily Record,* March 27, 1968.

Prater, Yvonne. "Early County Log Drives." Ellensburg, Wash., *Daily Record* (3-article series), November 20, 21, December 1, 1972.
Prater, Yvonne. "Snoqualmie Area Bridge Work Quiets for Winter." Ellensburg, Wash., *Daily Record*, November 29, 1978.
Relander, Click. "Winter Route over Cascades Found Up Yakima River." Yakima, Wash., *Herald-Republic,* June 30, 1960.
Rhodes, Elizabeth. "37 Odd and Almost Unheard of Facts about Seattle." *Seattle Times,* August 24, 1980.
Ruppert, Ray. "Father Egan Shares Long Study of Valley Names." Yakima, Wash., *Herald-Republic,* no date, from Yakima Valley Museum files.
Swergal, Edwin. "Lt. Tinkham Sees It Through." Spokane, Wash., *Spokesman-Review,* June 22, 1952.

V. Anonymous Newspaper Articles

Cle Elum, Washington, *Echo:*
   "Making Plans for Northwest Trail." January 23, 1915.
   "Governor Signs Highway Bill." March 12, 1915.
   "Came Through the Pass." April 25, 1915.
   "First Machine Via Snoqualmie." April 25, 1915.
   "Snoqualmie Pass Road Delayed." May 28, 1915.
   "Racing Auto Has Accident." June 25, 1915.
   "Chicago-Seattle Relay Race." June 25, 1915.
   "Sunset Highway is Dedicated." July 2, 1915.
   "Blazing the Red Trail." September 10, 1915.
   "Cle Elum on Yellow Trail." September 24, 1915.
   "Ellensburg Entertains Road Men." October 29, 1915.
   "Red Trail Man Seeks Some City Money." November 12, 1915.
   "Bids Let for Easton-Cle Elum Road." January 28, 1916.
   "Worst Snow Storm in 30 Years Hits Entire Northwest." February 4, 1916.
   "Charcoal to Open Snoqualmie Pass." March 3, 1916.
   "Mules Come to Make Road for Automobiles." April 28, 1916.
   "Road to River to be Ready in Ten Days." April 28, 1916.
   "Snow Still Deep Over Mountain." May 26, 1916.
   "Keechelus is Coming to the Front Rapidly." August 11, 1916.
   "Supporters of Good Road are Now Organized." August 11, 1916.
   "Record Breaker Coming Through." September 15, 1916.
   "Samuel Hill Road Expert Makes Visit." September 22, 1916.
   "Snoqualmie Pass Still Full of Snow." June 1, 1917.
   "Set Sunday to Open Pass." June 22, 1917.
   "Sunset Road to Be Open Very Shortly." May 17, 1918.
   "Snoqualmie Pass is in Good Shape." June 6, 1919.
   "Scouting Party Passes Through City." October 10, 1919.
   "E.J. Chartrand of Doughnut Inn Gives Some Astonishing Figures From Actual Count." December 8, 1922.
   "The Yellowstone Trail." February 23, 1923.
   "Bucking the Winter Snows in Snoqualmie." December 14, 1923.
   "Traffic on the Sunset Highway." July 11, 1924.
   "Praises Public Camping Park." September 12, 1924.
   "Next Heavy Snowfall Will Signal Opening of Skiers' Playground Bowl at Hyak." December 3, 1937.
Ellensburg, Washington, *Capital:*
   "Is Some Railroad Doing It?" December 24, 1891
   "A Strong Effort Being Made to Have It Rebuilt." February 21, 1895.

"The First Trans-Mountain Auto Trip." July 5, 1905.
"The First Auto Over the Cascades." July 19, 1905.
"A Fine Mountain Road in Prospect." August 16, 1905.
"Working Up Interest in Good Roads." July 29, 1908.
"Interest in Auto Race." June 25, 1909.
"Greatest Snowstorm Known in Years Has Raged in the Cascades." February 25, 1910.
"Greatest Storm on Record is Over." March 4, 1910.
"Snoqualmie Road Be Great Highway." April 29, 1910.
"Milwaukee Photo Car." May 27, 1910.
"Horse Round Up for Sound Market." June 22, 1911.
"County Men Forming a Club." April 11, 1912.
"Ellensburg is Hub of New Trunk Roads." May 23, 1912.
"Great Interest in Snoqualmie Road." July 11, 1912.
"Snoqualmie Road Ready for Traffic." July 18, 1912.
"Snoqualmie Road Gets Endorsement." September 12, 1912.
"Snoqualmie Road Gets a Big Boost." October 31, 1912.
"Two Men Drove Motorcycles Over." August 21, 1913.
"Motorists Preferred Shipping Machines Over Summit." November 27, 1913.
"Austin Mires Tells of Early Days." July 21, August 7, August 14, 1931.

Ellensburg, Washington, *Record:*
"Good Roads Men Meet January 20." January 11, 1910.
"Want State Route Changed." January 17, 1910.
"Hold a State Road Meeting Tonight." January 25, 1910.
"Convention Favors Snoqualmie Road." March 3, 1910.
"Milwaukee Line is Completely Tied Up." March 7, 1910.
"Traffic on the Milwaukee Opened." March 9, 1910.
"Engineer Tells of Milwaukee Construction." July 6, 1953.
"Cost Milwaukee Railroad $6,500,000 to Build Track Across Kittitas County Originally Before Electrifying Line." July 6, 1953.
"Quite an Experience Says Lost Paratrooper After Walking to Safety from Deep in Mountains." December 23, 1955.
"Local History Evident Along I-90." September 4, 1970.
"I-82 Leads To . . ." November 11, 1971.
"Wheelers and Dealers." January 26, 1972.
"From Puget Sound to the Upper Columbia — a 10 day trip in 1884." June 5, 1972. Reprinted from an 1884 article by Eugene Smalley in *The Century Magazine.*
"Seattle and Walla Walla Trail and Wagon Road." July, Bicentennial Edition, 1976.
"Toll Road Marker — 1940." February 4, 1976.
"Big Development Proposed." June 17, 1977.
"Commissioners Vote Monday on Big Summit Development." August 9, 1977.
"Rare Mastodon Remains Discovered in Peat Bog." August 24, 1977.
"Local Road Plans Explained." May 10, 1978.
"Snoqualmie Pass Problems Wrestled." June 14, 1978.
"They're Ready for Snow." October 26, 1978.
"Advisory System Improved." December 28, 1978.
"Snow Blocks Snoqualmie Pass." January 2, 1980.
"Merger Makes Ski Lift Biggest." August 23, 1980.

Olympia, Washington, *Pioneer and Democrat:* "Report of Committee Regarding Construction of Wagon Road." November 11, 1859.

Olympia, Washington, *Washington Standard:* "Snoqualmie Pass Completed." September 14, 1867.

Roslyn, Washington, *Sentinel:* Numerous articles. Souvenir Edition available from Roslyn Museum. March 1, 1895.

Seattle, Washington, *Gazette:* "Wagon Road Over the Cascades." August 27, 1864. "The Cascades Road Again." July 29, 1865.

Seattle, Washington, *Post-Intelligencer:* "Famous Old Wagon Road Thoroughfare over Snoqualmie Pass to be Repaired." April 31, 1899. "Dream of 'City Street' Over Pass Realized." August 25, 1937. "County to Rehabilitate Landmarks." February 4, 1979.

Seattle Times: "Hikers Alert: Avalanche Danger Great in Springtime." May 18, 1978.

Seattle, Washington, *Weekly Intelligencer:* "A Public Letter from Lake Kitchelas." October 7, 1867.

Snoqualmie, Washington, *Valley Record:* "It W-W-Was S-S-So-Cold." January 4, 1979. "Ashes Found in Fall City Bridge." October 16, 1980.

Teanaway City, Washington, *Teanaway Bugle:* "Partners Wanted." January, 1886.

Walla Walla, Washington, *Union Bulletin:* "Opening of the Snoqualmie Road." July 27, 1872. "Prospectus of the Seattle and Walla Walla Company." August 30, 1873.

Yakima, Washington, *Herald-Republic:* "Cemeteries Tell Roslyn's Past." October 21, 1968.
"North on I-82. The Story of a New Highway," November 11, 1971.

VI. Miscellaneous Publications

The Mountaineer Annual, Seattle, Wash.:
"The Lodge," by Sidney V. Bryant, 1914.
"Climbs Around Snoqualmie Lodge," by H.R. Morgan, 1931.
"Happiness is Skiing at Meany... ," 1968.

VII. Special Collections

"The Seattle and Walla Walla Trail and Wagon Road" by Larry Nickel, Ellensburg Library Local History Collection, Ellensburg, Wash.

"Concerning the Snoqualmie Pass Road" (A chronology.) by Ada S. Hill. Snoqualmie Valley Historical Museum, North Bend, Wash.

National Register of Historic Places Inventory-Nomination Records. From Washington State Historical Library, Tacoma, Wash.
"Renton Coal Hoist Foundation," August 1, 1975.
"The Old Red Brick Road (The Old Yellowstone Road)," July 31, 1974.
"Marymoor Farm Dutch Windmill," December 26, 1972.

"Che-ho-lan," a description by Theresa Smythe, Ellensburg Library Local History Collection.

"Bicentennial Calendar 1976." Ellensburg, Wash., Bicentennial Committee.

"The Upper County Heritage Council Bicentennial Commemorative Calendar" (for Cle Elum-Roslyn-Ronald-Easton). Upper County Heritage Council.

"Washington State Register of Historic Places." Office of Archaeology and Historic Preservation, Olympia, Wash.

"National Register (of Historic Places) Listing Through December, 1980." Office of Archaeology and Historic Preservation, Olympia, Wash.

1854 copy of handwritten letter from Abiel Tinkham from the National Archives, Topographical Engineers, Vol. 4, p. 585. (Polar File)

"Snoqualmie Pass Road Across the Mountains" by John W. Guye. University of

BIBLIOGRAPHY 161

Washington, Northwest Collection, Suzzallo Library, Seattle.

"Ordinance 104." An ordinance regulating the speed and operation of automobiles and other vehicles; laws that went into effect in Ellensburg, June 17, 1907. Ellensburg, Wash., Library, Local History Collection.

The Frank Streamer Papers. Washington State Historical Society Library, Tacoma, Wash.

Meadowbrook Hotel Register (from May 1888 to summer season of 1904), North Bend, Wash., Museum.

Keechelus Dam Construction Scrapbooks, U.S. Bureau of Reclamation Office, Yakima, Wash.

U.S. Forest Service Ranger Diaries for Easton in 1915 and 1924; Keechelus 1915, and Meadow Creek, 1924.

VIII. Maps

Cedar Lake Quadrangle, U.S. Geological Survey, 1913.

Map of a Part of Washington Territory, compiled by order of Lt. Col. Casey, U.S. Army, by Lt. G.H. Mendell, Topographic Engineer and George Gibbs, Engineer, 1856.

Map of State of Oregon and Washington Territory, compiled in the Bureau of Topographic Engineering, chiefly for military purposes by order of the Honorable John B. Floyd, Secretary of War, 1859.

Map of the State of Washington, Joseph Snow, Highway Commissioner, 1909.

Map of the State of Washington, W.J. Roberts, Highway Commissioner, 1912.

Map of the Territory of Oregon, West of the Rocky Mountains, compiled in the Bureau of Topographic Engineers, under the direction of Col. J.J. Abert, 1838.

Map of the Territory of the U.S. from the Mississippi to the Pacific Ocean, ordered by the Honorable Jefferson Davis, Secretary of War, to accompany the Reports of the Explorations for a Railroad Route in 1854.

Map of Territory of Washington, Records of the Department of Interior, 1876.

North Bend Recreation Area, Guide No. 29, Department of Agriculture, Snoqualmie National Forest, 1938.

Official Washington State Highway Map and Guide, Washington State Department of Transportation, 1979.

Rainier National Forest, U.S. Department of Agriculture, Forest Service, 1923.

Snoqualmie Pass Quadrangle, U.S. Geological Survey, Department of the Interior, 1901.

Snoqualmie Pass Quadrangle, U.S. Geological Survey, 1909.

Snoqualmie Pass Region, prepared by The Mountaineers, Seattle, 1917.

Snoqualmie Pass, Wa., Green Trails, No. 207, Bellevue, Wash.

State of Washington Highway Map, Samuel Humes, Highway Commissioner, 1928.

U.S. Geological Survey, Snoqualmie Quadrangle, Department of the Interior, 1961.

Yakima County, Washington Postal Service — Past and Present 1860-1974, by George Martin, Yakima, Wash., 1974.

Yellowstone Trail: A Good Road from Plymouth Rock to Puget Sound, published by the Yellowstone Highway Assn., Inc., Ipswich, S. Dak.

Names applied to the transportation route through Snoqualmie Pass:

Indian Trail
The Foot Trail
Packer's Trail
Hudson Bay Trail
Military Trail
Cattle Trail
Freight Trail
Miner's Trail
Pioneer Wagon Road
Hudson's Bay Packers Trail
Citizen's Road
Turnpike
Old Military Road
Territorial Road
Government Trail
People's Highway
Jerry Borst's Trail
The Cattlemen's Trail
State Wagon Road
County Wagon Road
State Wagon Road #7
State Road #7
Sunset Highway
Serpentine Trail
  (because of switchbacks)
Yellowstone Trail
Yellowstone Highway
The Transcontinental Route
The Red Trail
The National Parks Highway
The National Park Route
Private Toll Road
Seattle, Walla Walla Trail and
  Wagon Road
Seattle-Walla Walla Wagon Road
Seattle-Fort Colville Wagon Road
The Big Road
Highway 10
Interstate 90
The Oregon Trail
The Snoqualmie Pass Route
The Seattle-Spokane Highway
The Snoqualmie Pass Highway
The Wonder Route
The Scenic Route
The Mountain Highway
The Gateway to Puget Sound
The Gateway to the Inland Empire
The gap at Snoqualmie Pass
The Hill
Livestock Trail
The Washington Loop Highway

INDEX

Author **Yvonne Prater** is a resident of Ellensburg WA, where she has been a contributing writer for the *Ellensburg Record* and a variety of outdoor publications. She graduated from Central Washington University in 1995, and has taught at City University and for the Pacific Northwest Field Seminars. She received an award from Warner Pacific College for writing this history.

A frequent traveler through Snoqualmie Pass, Prater combined extensive formal research with interviews of old-timers, and spent months sifting through family albums and personal records to gather facts for this, her first book.

Author Yvonne Prater at Snoqualmie Pass; Guy Peak in the background.
Photo by Debbie Storlie.